WE WERE
CHAMPIONS

THE 49ERS' DYNASTY IN THEIR OWN WORDS

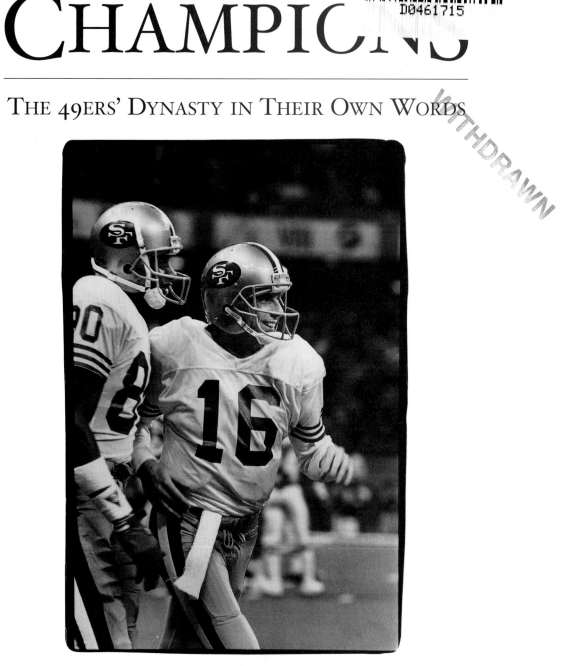

TRIUMPH
BOOKS
CHICAGO

WE WERE
CHAMPIONS

THE 49ERS' DYNASTY IN THEIR OWN WORDS

TEXT BY PHIL BARBER
PHOTOGRAPHY BY MICHAEL ZAGARIS

WE WERE CHAMPIONS
THE 49ERS' DYNASTY IN THEIR OWN WORDS

This book is available in quantity at special discounts for your group or organization. For further information, contact:
TRIUMPH BOOKS
601 South LaSalle Street, Suite 500
Chicago, Illinois 60605
Phone (312) 939-3330 FAX (312) 663-3557
Printed in the United States of America
ISBN 1-57243-498-8
TEXT BY PHIL BARBER
PHOTOGRAPHS BY MICHAEL ZAGARIS
BOOK DESIGN BY EVELYN JAVIER
EDITED BY TOM BARNIDGE

Library of Congress Cataloging-in-Publication Data
Barber, Phil.
    We were champions : the 49ers' dynasty in their own words / [text by Phil Barber ; photographs by Michael Zagaris].
        p. cm.
    Includes index.
    ISBN 1-57243-498-8 (hard)
    1. San Francisco 49ers (Football team) I. Zagaris, Michael. II. San Francisco 49ers (Football team) III. Title.

GV956.S3 B37 2002
796.332'64'0979461—dc21

2002071962

ON THE PRECEDING PAGES:

(1)   Jerry Rice and Joe Montana had reason to smile in Super Bowl XXIV, a 55-10 victory over the Denver Broncos.

(2-3) Keena Turner, Hacksaw Reynolds, and Ronnie Lott made defensive adjustments on the sidelines in 1984.

(4-5) The 49ers' defense celebrated a pivotal goal-line stand en route to victory over Cincinnati in Super Bowl XVI.

(6-7) Owner Eddie DeBartolo Jr., drenched in a locker-room celebration, relished a come-from-behind victory in Super Bowl XXIII.

(8-9) Coach Bill Walsh and quarterback Joe Montana plot fourth-quarter strategy in the 1984 NFC Championship Game.

CONTENTS

WE'LL BE CHAMPIONS AGAIN
BY BILL WALSH

Someday I'll take the time to sit back and consider what we accomplished in San Francisco. Maybe I'll watch a stack of old highlight tapes.

It's not that I'm blind to our achievements. The development, refinement, and practical application of our offensive system has give me much pride. Virtually every team in the league has utilized some form of our West Coast offense. We located and developed the ideal athletes to execute our system. We were a precision force, and the legacy lives on today with head coach Steve Mariucci and his staff.

Certainly, when I bump into Joe Montana or Ronnie Lott or George Seifert, one of us inevitably brings up some particularly humorous or intense memory—a championship game against Chicago or offensive tackle Bubba Paris trying to make weight. But I honestly don't dwell on the past. I've always been too busy. I still am.

You may have noticed that the 49ers are rolling again, fielding one of the best young teams in the league. I can't take full credit for that, of course, but I'm still part of the process in Santa Clara, and it's just as exhilarating as ever. To see a young quarterback such as Jeff Garcia—who grew up about 35 miles from our current headquarters, and who was virtually unwanted coming out of college—blossom in our system is extremely gratifying.

Jeff isn't the only talented player on the 49ers' current roster. I think our depth is as good as it has been for quite some time, and only a couple of our current players were with us for our last Super Bowl in 1994.

And yet, there is obvious continuity from the so-called glory days.

If I need an expert opinion on contract negotiations or the salary cap, I can walk down the hallway and talk to my old friend John McVay. He was a key member of our front office throughout the dynasty years, and he's still a vital link. Two doors down from John is Bill McPherson, our director of pro personnel. Bill was on our staff as a defensive coach during all five of our Super Bowl seasons. Our current coaching staff includes former players Dwaine Board (defensive line) and Tom Rathman (running backs). Dwaine came to the 49ers the same year I did; I drafted Tom in 1986. Between them they played 18 seasons here and earned five Super Bowl rings. Our trainer Lindsy McLean has been here since 1979, and our physical development coordinator, Jerry Attaway, has been around since 1983. Former linebacker Keena Turner is our player development director, and his alumni coordinators include such memorable contributors as Guy McIntyre, Jesse Sapolu, and Eric Wright, all members of 49ers Super Bowl teams.

Even Bobb McKittrick's presence remains. Bobb was one of my dearest friends in the world and an absolutely brilliant offensive line coach. After he finally lost his battle with cancer in 2000, the club kept his practice locker intact. I can go down and look at it any time for inspiration.

Believe me, the 49ers aren't living in the past. It's important that young players such as Jeff Garcia, Terrell Owens, and Andre Carter develop their own reputations and register their own victories. All of us in the front office and on the coaching staff are wholly focused on supporting them. But I think that today's achievements are made possible by what was built here during the last 20-plus years.

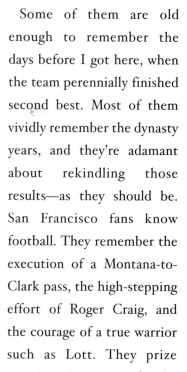

I look back fondly at certain games, certain moments on the field. But what I'm most proud of is the underlying foundation that made it all possible. That is our true legacy.

Whether looking for a free safety or an assistant coach or an accountant, we always tried to find people with character—bright, energetic people who were willing to sacrifice and able to work independently. I think we were remarkably successful in finding this sort of person, from top to bottom. Once we did, the organization sort of took on a life of its own. It became bigger than any one of us. That's why the 49ers continued to win when I stepped down in 1989, and when Ronnie Lott went to the Raiders in 1991, and when Joe Montana went to Kansas City in 1993. It's why the 49ers are winning again.

There is one other source of continuity I have neglected to mention. That is the 49ers' fans.

Some of them are old enough to remember the days before I got here, when the team perennially finished second best. Most of them vividly remember the dynasty years, and they're adamant about rekindling those results—as they should be. San Francisco fans know football. They remember the execution of a Montana-to-Clark pass, the high-stepping effort of Roger Craig, and the courage of a true warrior such as Lott. They prize excellence, and this, too, is an inspiration for the current crop of 49ers.

As I said, I've never been one to sit back to try to grasp the big picture of what we did here between 1981 and 1994. I'll leave that to our fans. I just hope they don't leave themselves out of the equation because we couldn't have done it without them.

THE STORYTELLERS

The players, coaches, and club personnel listed below and quoted on the following pages all played a part in creating one of the NFL's most enduring dynasties. They remain linked to a memorable era in San Francisco 49ers history, during which a franchise that never before had won a championship claimed five Super Bowl titles.

HARRIS BARTON: An offensive lineman for the 49ers from 1987-1998 who started at right tackle in three Super Bowls (XXIII, XXIV, and XXIX).

DWIGHT CLARK: A wide receiver for the 49ers from 1979-1987, best remembered for making "The Catch" against the Dallas Cowboys in the 1981 NFC title game; he started in Super Bowls XVI and XIX. After retiring, he spent 10 years (1988-1997) as a 49ers administrator, rising to the position of vice president/director of football operations.

ROGER CRAIG: A running back for the 49ers from 1983-1990 who started in Super Bowls XIX, XXIII, and XXIV. He also played for the Los Angeles Raiders (1991) and Minnesota Vikings (1992-93).

RANDY CROSS: An offensive lineman for the 49ers from 1976-1988 who started at right guard in Super Bowls XVI and XIX and at center in Super Bowl XXIII.

EDDIE DEBARTOLO JR.: The owner of the 49ers from 1977-1997.

KEITH FAHNHORST: An offensive lineman for the 49ers from 1974-1987 who started at right tackle in Super Bowls XVI and XIX.

DWIGHT HICKS: A safety for the 49ers from 1979-1985 who started in Super Bowls XVI and XIX. He also played for the Indianapolis Colts (1986).

BRENT JONES: A tight end for the 49ers from 1987-1997 who played in Super Bowl XXIII and started in Super Bowls XXIV and XXIX.

RONNIE LOTT: A defensive back for the 49ers from 1981-1990 who started at cornerback in Super Bowls XVI and XIX and at safety in XXIII and XXIV. He also played for the Los Angeles Raiders (1991-92) and the New York Jets (1993-94).

GUY MCINTYRE: An offensive lineman for the 49ers from 1984-1993 who played in Super Bowl XIX, started at right guard in Super Bowl XXIII and at left guard in Super Bowl XXIV. He also played for the Green Bay Packers (1994) and Philadelphia Eagles (1995-96).

BILL MCPHERSON: An assistant coach (linebackers/defensive line/defensive coordinator) with the 49ers from 1979-1998; he has served as director of pro personnel since 1999.

JOHN MCVAY: A key member of the 49ers' front office (general manager/director of player personnel/director of football operations/vice president) from 1979-1995; he returned in 1998 as vice president/director of football operations.

MATT MILLEN: A linebacker for the 49ers from 1989-1990 who started in Super Bowl XXIV. He also played for the Oakland Raiders (1980-81), Los Angeles Raiders (1982-88), and Washington Redskins (1991).

JOE MONTANA: A quarterback for the 49ers from 1979-1992 who started in Super Bowls XVI, XIX, XXIII, and XXIV, earning MVP honors three times. He finished his career with the Kansas City Chiefs (1993-94).

CARMEN POLICY: A key member of the 49ers' front office who served as general counsel (1983-88), executive vice president (1989-1990), and president (1991-98).

JESSE SAPOLU: An offensive lineman for the 49ers from 1983-1997 who started at left guard in Super Bowls XXIII and XXIX and at center in Super Bowl XXIV. He was injured for XIX.

FREDDIE SOLOMON: A wide receiver for the 49ers from 1978-1985 who started in Super Bowls XVI and XIX. He also played for the Miami Dolphins (1975-77).

KEENA TURNER: A linebacker for the 49ers from 1980-1990 who started in Super Bowls XVI, XIX, XXIII, and XXIV.

BILL WALSH: Head coach of the 49ers from 1979-1988, during which they won six NFC West titles and Super Bowls XVI, XIX, and XXIII; he retired with a career record of 102-63-1. He returned to the organization as general manager in 1999 and now serves as a consultant.

MIKE WALTER: A linebacker for the 49ers from 1984-1993 who played in Super Bowl XIX and started in Super Bowls XXIII and XXIV. He also played for Dallas (1983).

ERIC WRIGHT: A defensive back for the 49ers from 1981-1990 who started in Super Bowls XVI and XIX and played in Super Bowls XXIII and XXIV.

MICHAEL ZAGARIS: The 49ers' team photographer who has been working for the club since 1973.

CHAPTER ONE

BIRTH OF A DYNASTY

he San Francisco 49ers weren't exactly a laughingstock during their first three decades of football. They had, in fact, been the second-best team in the All-America Football Conference (a notch or two behind the Cleveland Browns) throughout the league's brief existence (1946-49). They had finished with a winning record more often than not in their subsequent years in the NFL, and had captured three consecutive NFC Western Division titles from 1970-72.

But in all their years under the ownership of the popular Morabito family—first Anthony, then his brother Vic, then their widows, Josephine and Jane—the 49ers never won a league championship. Thirty-one seasons had come and gone by the time Edward DeBartolo Jr. purchased the franchise on March 31, 1977.

DeBartolo, who had been born in Youngstown, Ohio, in 1946, was almost exactly as old as his new team. At 31, he was the youngest owner in the league. Perhaps it was youth that made him impatient. Or maybe it was the visible success enjoyed by his father, Eddie Sr., and the DeBartolo Corporation in its many real-estate development ventures. In any case, Eddie Jr. had no intention of waiting passively for good things to happen.

Not that DeBartolo immediately struck gold. Under his first general manager, Joe Thomas, the 49ers showed no signs of progress. It wasn't until 1979 and the arrival of Bill Walsh, the professorial coach from nearby Stanford, that the 49ers began to take shape as an emerging power. Even then, Walsh needed time to assemble the necessary talent.

Mike White (left) embraced Bill Walsh after his first victory with the 49ers.

BRENT JONES: Right about '73-'74, when I was really into my football heyday, the 49ers were pretty bad. I remember my parents got my brother a 49ers jacket. He was three years younger than me. The 49ers were terrible, and my brother cried. He wouldn't wear it to school. The 49ers stunk, so the jacket was never worn. And that's kind of how our family was. You didn't want to be associated with a loser, and they were losers.

EDDIE DEBARTOLO: I had a press conference just after the team was purchased. My message would probably fit right now, in today's day and age, but it wasn't accepted very well then, because I said that football's a business: "We're gonna do our best to make money and run it as a business." And I just about got run out of town on a rail. Some of the older players came to the press conference, and most of these guys were older than me. I mean, Cedrick Hardman and Tommy Hart and Gene Washington—they were either older than me or the same age.

RANDY CROSS: I worked for the Morabitos my first year. I was (eventually) the last player on our roster who was drafted by somebody other than a DeBartolo person. It was just a real old-style family NFL organization, and it was completely different. And it didn't get better right away. Eddie brought in Joe Thomas. He was to an NFL franchise what scorched earth is to landscaping. He wanted no part of any history....To some degree, you want to disas-

sociate yourself with any losing that had gone on in the past when you come in. But you lose a little piece of your soul when you say, "We want nothing to do with all those great years, all that rich tradition." It was a terrible time to be a 49er.

MICHAEL ZAGARIS: I've got a lot of the old bound volumes of the team (programs and guides) because I went in one day after Thomas took over. Dave Frei was the PR guy, and I saw all these programs and pictures, and the charter of the team, in boxes. And I said, "What are you doing with these? Taking these to Candlestick?"

And he said, "Oh, this stuff? We're taking it to the dump."

And I said, "No, seriously, what are you doing?"

He said, "Joe Thomas said, 'History begins today. Get all this crap out of here. We don't want any of this.'"

It was like the Visigoths coming in and sacking Rome. And I said, "Now wait a minute, are you telling me you're really taking this to the dump?"

And he said, "Yeah, they're coming to pick it up."

And I said, "Wow, what a small world, because I was actually on my way to the dump myself anyway to drop some other stuff. If you want, I'll take some of this for you."

He said, "Sure, help yourself."

So I grabbed a ton of stuff.

RANDY CROSS: We were 2-14 in 1978....I would nominate '78 as one of the worst teams to ever play

Steve DeBerg (left) held down the starting quarterback job before his unheralded backup, Joe Montana, emerged.

football. Easily. I put them up against anybody who won one (game), and I would give you the 49ers and a touchdown.

KEITH FAHNHORST: The lowest point might have been the last game of 1978. We were in Detroit for the last game of the year. Steve DeBerg got hurt. Whoever the next quarterback was (Scott Bull) got hurt. (Wide receiver) Freddie Solomon was put in at quarterback. He was running around like crazy, scrambling, trying to make plays. We were running around like crazy trying to block for him. And I remember after the game—Fred O'Connor was our coach at the time—he was talking about how things were gonna be different next year, and we were gonna have one of the toughest camps in the league. He was more or less gonna make men out of all of us. And I just thought, "Oh, lord, we don't need things to be tougher, we need things to be smarter."

EDDIE DEBARTOLO: We hired Kenny Meyer (as head coach in 1977). We went through a couple of coaches—(Pete McCulley and Fred O'Connor) in 1978. Then Bill came in, and I guess it was the start of—if you want to call it so—the dynasty....

We only had one interview. Bill Walsh was brought to my attention by a sports talk-show host out in the Bay Area by the name of Ron Barr....At that time we were floundering. The team wasn't playing very well. We had gone through our share of

coaches. Joe Thomas was no longer with us. I (was going to) let him go. And Bill and I agreed to meet.

BILL WALSH: I was pretty much at ease because I was extremely satisfied with my position at Stanford. We just had an excellent year, and we were having another one, so I didn't feel the pressure of a job interview.

EDDIE DEBARTOLO: We met at my room in the Fairmont Hotel in San Francisco. It was just the two of us....We talked about football, we talked about philosophy. We talked about family, about values. I don't think the meeting—I won't really call it an interview—took longer than 45 minutes. I just knew, after sitting with him, that he was the guy I wanted to bring the franchise back to some form of stability. I offered him the job.

BILL WALSH: Some of it was football. Some of it was me. Some of it was him. But I think we quickly had the same thing in mind. I became very enthusiastic about joining the 49ers, and it appeared he was really impressed in some way with me. So it didn't take a lengthy series of interviewing....Then it was for me to deal with Stanford for the remainder of the year—we had a bowl game coming up (Bluebonnet Bowl)—and for Eddie to deal with Joe Thomas in his own way.

It was soon thereafter, I believe, that I received a

Randy Cross, who joined the 49ers in 1976, remembered the early years as "a terrible time to be a 49er."

phone call. Eddie all but said he was going to do it. But then we had a bowl game. Eddie had all of his entourage—all of his friends—over for a New Year's Eve party, and he had the television on our game against Georgia. I was noted for having a feel for offensive football, and everybody was talking about it. So Georgia proceeded to just beat the hell out us in front of all Eddie's friends. They were ahead 22-0 in the middle of the third quarter. By that time, Eddie's friends had all left and gone up and danced and were enjoying themselves....

I was just praying on the sideline that we'd score a touchdown—just one touchdown, for God's sakes. Because I could see this 49ers thing maybe slipping away. And we took it away from Georgia and beat them pretty soundly in the fourth quarter and beat them 25-22. So I was sort of redeemed.

BILL MCPHERSON: Sometimes we brought in people on a Friday and they played for us on Sunday. If they were good, we kept them. If they weren't, we fired them and brought some more guys in the next week. I've told people over the years, in those days we almost brought them in by the busload. Or we went down to Harry's Hofbrau in Redwood City and said, "We need a corner for this game. You're up." At the cornerback position, for example, I think we might have gone through 20-odd players that first year (1979).

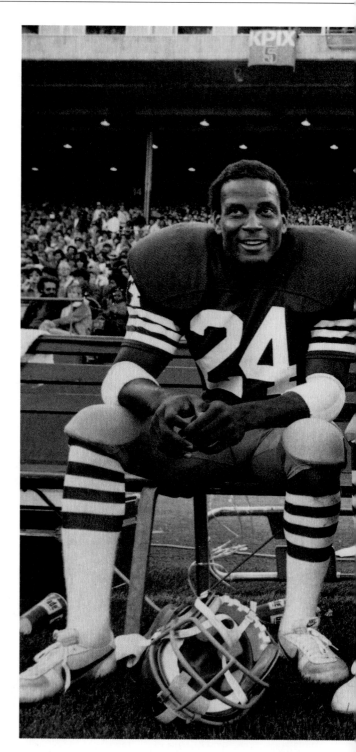

The 49ers' secondary received an injection of youth in 1981 with rookies Ronnie Lott, Eric Wright, and Carlton Williamson.

We had a veteran defensive lineman by the name of Cedrick Hardman, really a good player. We had so many new people coming in and out, I heard him say to one of the new players one time, "Hey, Brand New Man, line up over here." These guys were coming in and out so fast, they were there to get a cup of coffee and one practice and they were gone. During the season we're putting names on guys' helmets to know who we had.

RANDY CROSS: And then we proceeded to be the best 2-14 team ever. I guess my view was a little bit slanted in that I was an offensive player. We moved the ball. We scored points. We were kind of the reason people got excited for '80 and '81.

JOHN MCVAY: That first year, there were a lot of empty seats. I remember one time we had like an open-house promotion at the stadium. We were gonna call it "Pick Your Seat," but it had kind of a bad connotation so we called it "Select a Seat." We had a little band, a ragtime combo, and we were giving away free hot dogs and everything. We had people come in, and we had all the available seats marked. You can have all kinds of marketing devices, but the best marketing device is the success of the team. When the team started having success in '81, it sold out about the middle of the season, and it has ever since.

A packed house and the Goodyear blimp stared down on the 49ers as they prepared to take the field for a kickoff.

CHAPTER TWO

A PASSIONATE OWNER

dward DeBartolo Jr. had the weight of his father's financial empire behind him (Edward Sr. died in 1994). But when it came to running the 49ers, Junior called the shots. In doing so, he violated one of the cardinal rules of the sports business: Ownership and talent cannot be pals. But somehow it worked in San Francisco.

If DeBartolo was as close to his players as any owner ever dared be, he had the sense to leave the football decisions to Bill Walsh, John McVay, and other "football men."

Not that he was detached from the team. On the contrary, DeBartolo demanded results, and he could be as emotional as any fan in good times or bad.

Eddie Jr. helped to build a memorable dynasty, but he fell from grace in 1997. That was when the NFL suspended him for his role in a suspect arrangement involving casino licenses in Louisiana.

Ownership of the club eventually transferred to his sister, Denise DeBartolo York, and her husband, John York. The couple runs the 49ers today.

Ed DeBartolo Sr. rejoiced with Junior after the 1981 NFC Championship Game.

JOHN MCVAY: I remember one of the first times I met Senior, he said, "I want you to understand. I want everything first class. Everything."

"Yes, sir."

But that's the way it was done. It gave us the mandate. Just go out and do what you have to do to put the 49ers on top.

RANDY CROSS: It wasn't because we were paid the best, because there were teams that paid as well as the 49ers did. But you flew first class when you traveled. We took DC-10s and L-1011s and big stretches. We didn't cram into planes. They catered all our food on airplanes. We stayed in the best hotels.

That was always the number-one topic of conversation in the offseason, around guys who played on other teams, or at the Pro Bowl, or at the Super Bowl. Those stories about how fortunate we were got around quickly.

MICHAEL ZAGARIS: (DeBartolo) treated everyone equally. And when I say everyone, I mean from Joe Montana to the groundskeeper to the janitor. And me. Made us all feel like a family, and equal. If your child had graduated from school, whether grade school or high school, he'd send you a little note. If you wrote a great article, he'd send you a little note. If there was a death in your family, there'd be flowers and a personal note of condolence. There were bonuses to anyone and everyone. Even

the years we didn't win Super Bowls, that would still happen. There's a lot of talk in sports about family. But this really was a true family.

ERIC WRIGHT: He was like a friend and a big brother, and then he was your boss, too. He was shrewd at times. We're still good friends today....He's the only owner that I know. I'm here thinking all owners are like that, but no, there's only one Mr. D. When you were in a time of need, or your family had something wrong, he was there for you....Like Jeff Fuller. Jeff got partially paralyzed. Mr. D. took care of Jeff when he couldn't work. You don't hear about stuff like that.

BILL MCPHERSON: Dwaine Board had a bad ankle. Back then you had to expose an injured player on the waiver wire before you could re-activate him. We were playing the Saints the next week, and (New Orleans coach Jim Mora) claimed Dwaine to find out (about our game plan). And the damn guy told him. I wanted to kill him! We were down there at the game, and I asked John Pease, their defensive line coach—he's an old friend of mine—"Did Dwaine tell you anything?"

He said, "He told me everything."

That was a Super Bowl year. Eddie brought (Board) to the Super Bowl party and gave him a Super Bowl ring. How many guys would do that? That shows you what kind of a guy Eddie was.

The owner treated everyone equally, even blue-collar players such as defensive end Archie Reese (78) and linebacker Willie Harper.

DeBartolo and coach Bill Walsh relished an improbable, last-play victory over Cincinnati in 1987.

RANDY CROSS: He learned a lot from his father. I think a lot of what he did was a direct reflection of what Eddie Sr. did. He paid us the best, and he treated us the best, but he expected results. It was expected that if you didn't come through, there were going to be repercussions. But that was fine. We happened to have a group of people who thought, "Hey, no problem. If that's the deal, we'll just keep winning."

BILL McPHERSON: He put a lot of money into the club and allowed us to go out and get the players we needed. Like when we first started. You guys want Fred Dean? Go get him. You want Hacksaw Reynolds? Go get him. You want Big Hands Johnson and Louie Kelcher? Go get 'em. So he's spending a heck of a lot of money. In exchange, he wanted to see some results.

MICHAEL ZAGARIS: The Raiders came in and beat us (in 1988, dropping the 49ers to 6-5). And we came into the locker room after the game and found the glass broken on this soft-drink cooler. Mr. D was so pissed he had kicked a hole in it. He was very, very emotional. I mean, he lived and died for the team.

JOHN McVAY: When we lost, the DeBartolos were crushed. They were used to such enormous success in their business. So now, this is a different breed of cat. It took a little while to get used to it.

I almost got fired once. Eddie was at my house, and in my office I had a game ball from (1978) when I was coaching the Giants and we beat the 49ers. It was all painted up, "New York Giants beat the 49ers, such and such." He said, "What the hell is that doing up there?"

CARMEN POLICY: Eddie felt passionate about the team. He wanted the 49ers to be the standard. Whatever his shortcomings, all of us are thankful to him for the opportunity to have been a part of it.

JESSE SAPOLU: Eddie DeBartolo was probably the most generous owner in professional sports at the time. But at the same time, if we lost a game, he's probably the owner you'd least want to be around. He took care of you, but he expected you to win.

EDDIE DeBARTOLO: Ronnie (Lott) to this day will say he knows I was ready to suit up and go to war with them any time.

CHAPTER THREE

COACH AND VISIONARY

THE PRESENCE. HE HAD STYLE.

ill Walsh had apprenticed under some of football's most innovative minds, including Paul Brown, Al Davis, Sid Gillman (indirectly, at least), and Don Coryell. He also had led Stanford to a breakthrough season in 1977 and another successful year in 1978. Still, when Eddie DeBartolo hired him as head coach of the 49ers in 1979, Walsh had little in the way of a national reputation.

By the time he stepped down a decade later, the coach had earned 102 career victories and three Super Bowl trophies, not to mention the label of "genius." There is no denying Walsh's lasting impact on the game. His offense dismantled some of the best defenses in the NFL, and since has been copied and adapted by practically everyone.

Walsh's abilities weren't limited to the chalkboard, either. He was at the forefront of a scouting group that consistently uncovered NFL talent at small college programs (such as James Madison's Charles Haley) and in later rounds of the draft (Dwight Clark in the tenth, Jesse Sapolu in the eleventh). And those who worked closely with Walsh will tell you that his most important contributions were organizational. He had a visionary's sense of how a club should run, and he was detail oriented enough to make it all happen.

Working for Walsh was not always a comfortable proposition. He could be hard to please, and harder to read. These traits, combined with DeBartolo's volatility, made for some interesting moments between owner and coach.

From the first day of his first training camp, Bill Walsh clearly was in charge.

CARMEN POLICY: I met him at the second interview. The moment he walked in the room, you got the feeling that he had presence, that he had style. He seemed to have a sense of awareness of what was expected of him.

Now, you can be fooled. With some people, the book looks great, but beyond the preface there's no substance to the text. In Bill's case, the cover looked great, and the book was even better.

RANDY CROSS: Was I wary? Let's see, when he came in it was my fourth year. He was my fifth head coach. So *wary* would be a good word. *Skeptical* would be another good word. If you know you can play football, at some point your attitude toward a coach gets to be, "Let's see how *you* do."...

His first speech got everybody's undivided attention. He made the point that, "You guys are sitting out there waiting on me and figure, 'Hey, look, if I can't play for this guy, I'll go play somewhere else.'" He says, "In case you haven't kept up on current events, this is the worst team in the NFL. If you can't play for me, who else can you play for?"

JOHN McVAY: Hiring Bill was the key to getting the thing started. Bill was not only the coach, he was the general manager. And shortly thereafter he was the president. So he was the true representative of the ownership.

BILL WALSH: It started with Ed and me agreeing that we needed a general manager, and that I would be the coach, and I would have responsibility for all personnel decisions. But we needed a general manager for all kinds of reasons, business-wise and other. I talked to a number of top people who turned the job down—George Young being one of them, Ernie Accorsi being another. These are all people I talked to about being the general manager of the 49ers. And to a man they turned it down....Because, to be honest, they didn't think it had a chance....

So sitting one day with Eddie and Carmen Policy, we looked at each other and I said, "Well, I guess I should be general manager."

And they said, "Whew, we've been waiting for you to say that."...

As for becoming president, I think we had won a Super Bowl and Eddie made me president. But that really didn't have any effect at all on anything.

RANDY CROSS: Bill set the standard....I don't care if you were answering a telephone, taking clothes out of a dryer, breaking down tapes, throwing touchdowns, getting interceptions. I mean there was an expected way of how you dealt with the public and how you did your job. It was easily the most underappreciated part of what he did.

BILL McPHERSON: Bill pretty much cleared out the whole building when he took over. He didn't just change some players. He changed the front-office staff, he and Mr. DeBartolo. I think even the lady at the switchboard left, and the guys taking care of the grounds.

Walsh made some minor tweaks to his offense at halftime of a 35-8 victory over the Washington Redskins in 1985.

EDDIE DeBARTOLO: He had an eye, not just for football talent but for administrative talent. The way he was able to handle people was unparalleled, and that was the basis for the success.

CARMEN POLICY: He was able to evaluate players on his own, or take reference points from a scout's evaluation, or from assistant coaches. He could draw out the most valuable aspect of an evaluation, and leave behind the more irrelevant or damaging aspects. He didn't ignore shortcomings. But he was not always confined in the same box as others. He could see great athletes from small programs.

MIKE WALTER: (During my senior year), Coach Walsh actually came to (the University of Oregon in) Eugene. He came down to Autzen Stadium, late at night. I was the last guy in the weight room and he came down and met me there, just kind of talked to me while I lifted weights. We went out and he

The coach shared pointers with three of his primary weapons: Dwight Clark, Freddie Solomon, and Joe Montana.

With all preparations tended to in the waning moments until game time, the coach found a place to relax before Super Bowl XXIII.

kind of watched me run around the field—not so much finding out what I could do athletically, more just kind of talking to me. I think just finding out what kind of person I was. He really impressed me in that way.

KEENA TURNER: Bill had his way and his plan and his vision about it, and his expectation level, not just what he saw (for) the team and himself, but for everybody else individually. And I think because

he's a very broad thinker, sometimes it's hard to condense that down to the one on one, because he's thinking of so many different elements of it....So as a player, there was always a feeling of some distance. And there was always the feeling of being just a little bit off balance. You did have times when you were really wondering what he was thinking.

I think a lot of those things were on purpose because Bill realized that the nature of people and what we do in this business isn't natural. The greatness really is only attained on the edge. He kept himself on a certain edge, and he kept us on a certain edge.

DWIGHT CLARK: I think some of his personality was formed when he didn't get the (head-coaching) job in Cincinnati. Paul Brown said he was too close to the players, and they chose to go with Bill Johnson as the head coach (in 1976) instead of Bill Walsh. I think he, at that point, changed his relationship with players. And that's too bad because you could tell he loved the players. He loved being around them. There was one time in the training room where I'm walking through there, and he wanted to say something to me, and he called me by my first name. Then he corrected himself and started calling me Clark, almost to distance himself from me.

KEITH FAHNHORST: I think Bill was not an easy guy to work for....We were playing the Bears in the '84 playoffs to get to the Super Bowl, and Bill was real nervous about it. So he came to the captains. We were supposed to have a day off the next day, and he said that he'd like to have us come in and practice and have a regular day, just because of the importance of the game. Well, the assistant coaches were aware that he was gonna do this. So they came to the captains and asked us to tell Bill that

Even on an afternoon in 1984 when victory at Atlanta was near, Walsh strolled the sideline, preoccupied with Xs and Os.

we'd rather not come in. Because they didn't really want us in. They wanted to get the game plan prepared and everything. But as good a coach as Bill was, he was pretty demanding. So they thought it would be easier for the players to say "let's not come in" than the coaches to say "let's not come in." So we were prepared for Bill, and we politely said we didn't think it would be a good idea. Bill listened to us. Bill was good that way.

EDDIE DEBARTOLO: All these writers write about the arguments we had, that he had this, that, and everything else, and he was fired. In the 10 years we were together as owner and coach, I don't think we exchanged more than two cross words. He was never fired....I talked to him less than a week ago. He's got a little vineyard in his backyard, and he's sending me some wine.

JOHN MCVAY: Whenever you have two highly successful, strong-willed, personable guys, you're gonna have hard discussions. I don't recall them ever being in a situation where it was acrimonious or ugly. I never remember either DeBartolo, Eddie or his dad, calling and saying, "Hey, why don't you play Smith?" There was never that kind of pressure.

DWIGHT CLARK: When it comes to football, I still hang on to what he preached. I'm writing a memo right now to everybody (in the Cleveland Browns' organization) to "cut down the distractions to the players, no fraternizing with the players, stay out of their way, let's get 'em what they need to win, we're here to support them, it's not about us, it's about the players and the coaches."...And that's one of the many things I got from Bill Walsh.

ROGER CRAIG: I think what Bill Walsh created has definitely given us life skills outside the game. I worked for his software company. It's called Tibco Software company. And I used our same strategies that we did when I was with the 49ers. How we set up meetings and what I ask of our sales team, how to work together, be an extension of each other, things like that.

BILL MCPHERSON: I have the opportunity every Monday to show him the film of our game. It's a clinic. He'll draw some plays. Then he visits the offensive guys and says, "Hey, I've got a couple of ideas." He can sit down and think about one play, while he's drawing another play, and then boom. The other day he had five pages of plays. How many guys in this business have actually invented something? Not many.

The 49ers never had played in the Super Bowl before the arrival of Walsh, who directed the team to three championships in 10 seasons.

CHAPTER FOUR

AMERICA'S FAVORITE QUARTERBACK

hen Joe Montana joined the 49ers as a rookie from Notre Dame in 1979, fellow draftee Dwight Clark mistook him for a free-agent kicker. Who wouldn't? By NFL standards, Montana looked a bit fragile, and his unassuming demeanor hardly demanded attention.

But it didn't take the 49ers long to realize that Montana's fluid mechanics, mobility, field vision, and split-second decision making made him the perfect quarterback for Bill Walsh's system. As good as he was in normal circumstances—his passer rating of 92.3 ranks second in NFL history, behind Steve Young—

the ultra-competitive Montana was at his best when it mattered most. From the 1981 NFC Championship Game to Super Bowl XXIII (in January, 1989) and beyond, he continually came up with clock-beating heroics. A three-time Super Bowl MVP, Montana threw 122 passes without an interception in the big game.

Both Walsh and his quarterback acknowledge that they didn't always see eye to eye, but they complemented one another to a rare degree. Meanwhile, Montana's easy smile and quiet charisma made him a leader of teammates and an undying legend among NFL fans.

Joe Montana possessed a rare knack for playing his best when it mattered most.

JOHN MCVAY: We got him in the third round with a pick we got in a trade (Dallas via Seattle). We didn't even have a first-round pick in '79 because of the O.J. trade (the 49ers acquired Simpson from Buffalo for five draft choices). In the second round, we took a running back named (James) Owens. Good kid, tried hard, was really fast, but football just wasn't his thing. Then we got Joe.

BILL WALSH: We had Steve DeBerg, who was performing pretty darn well the first year. He broke a record for completions (347 in 1979) and he played well. He wasn't very mobile, and that hurt us. But he was a good performer. Of course, he played for 17 years. But Joe was there, and every time Joe played it was absolutely exhilarating. Fortunately, because of Steve, I was able to use Joe at appropriate times in a game. And we didn't feel the heat of having to win.

JOHN MCVAY: (Walsh) essentially spoon-fed Joe. I mean, he didn't just say, "Get in there." He had other quarterbacks who played, and played well, in the system.

KEITH FAHNHORST: We were in St. Louis when Joe got his first start (on December 2, 1979). He was nervous, obviously, and kind of stumbled around in

The quarterback was low key, even whimsical, off the field, but he took charge of the offense once the game began.

the huddle, trying to call plays. And I just thought, "This'll never work. Here we go again."

Even during the '81 season, you saw great moments with Joe, but you didn't really see the kind of character that suggested he could handle pressure the way he did until we got to the playoffs. It was almost like Joe would be bored with games unless there was a lot on the line....The more pressure, the better he played. Most people don't function that way.

DWIGHT CLARK: Once practice started, if Joe needed to be assertive he would. But he really could flip a switch when a game started. It's almost like he could even take it to another level under intense pressure.

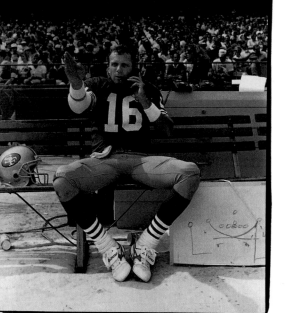

BILL WALSH: Joe began to demonstrate things that, once he learned the offense, were just ideally suited for what we wanted and what he wanted. We could have made it without Joe. I'm sure we'd have won Super Bowls without Joe Montana, (though) I don't know when they would have been. On the other hand, Joe was the team. He was the singular person who took us where we got to.

KEITH FAHNHORST: Football fans always talk about certain quarterbacks and how good they are. There's never gonna be another Joe Montana, and nobody even came close to him. I live in Minnesota. I hear about Fran Tarkenton. And it's a joke to compare Fran to Joe.

DWIGHT CLARK: He was much less of a take-charge guy off the field. He was still very calm off the field, and great under pressure if something should come up. But he was quiet. He was a jokester. He loved practical jokes—loved 'em—he would get somebody every chance he got.

He used to take George (Seifert's) bike. We'd come out of our meeting, and if George was still in

A bruised knee didn't dampen Montana's spirits in 1987 as he talked with Eddie DeBartolo after a 41-0 victory over the Bears.

a meeting, Joe would take his bike and ride it back down to the dorm and leave it there. He put somebody's bike on top of a tree, right outside the meeting room. He chained all the bikes together one time. He was notorious at training camp. That's where he did most of his real good work. Then once the season started it was time to get a little bit serious. But even then he was really good at keeping people relaxed.

GUY McINTYRE: He was great at keeping up morale. Even if the center had a bad snap or something, he'd say, "It was my fault." Like at practice: "It was my fault. I pulled out too soon." Or if somebody missed the pass, he'd say, "I'll hit you better next time. I'll get you in the right spot." Or if you (gave up) a sack, he'd say, "I'm all right."

BILL WALSH: Joe treated everyone as an equal—the lowest rookie or the owner. Didn't matter. Everyone, in Joe's mind, was a person. And that was one of Joe's great strengths. So the players responded to him.

JOE MONTANA: The longer you work with someone, sometimes the more difficult it becomes. Because you almost know what the other person is thinking. He knows what you want to do, and you know what he wants to do, and you know what's

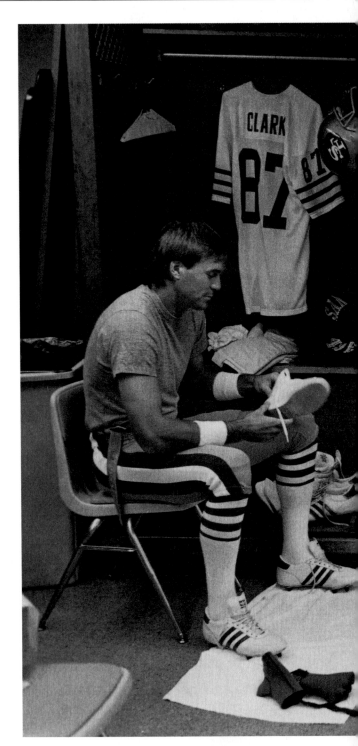

Wide receiver Dwight Clark and Montana, next-door locker mates, relaxed in the moments before a 1985 game against the Rams.

gonna be done. But I don't ever remember there being any real problem between Bill and me.

DWIGHT CLARK: Bill and Joe are both brilliant football minds, so there's gonna be a clash of ideas about the right plays to call. But as far as the relationship that a head coach—especially an offensive-minded head coach—and a quarterback have, I think it was better than most....

Joe would get pissed off at Bill and I'm sure Bill would get pissed off at Joe. Joe would change a play, audible to something that Bill didn't think should have been called. And I know for a fact that Joe would get upset in the huddle when something would come in that didn't sound right to him. Because you'd hear about it in the huddle. And there were a few times as Joe came off the field that he would walk by Bill, and they would banter back and forth with language that probably wasn't fit for family television. But it's football. It's a volatile sport. Both are just highly competitive and trying to figure out how to win.

JOE MONTANA: As far as play calling, I could have thrown the ball every down. Bill knows it. He probably would have liked to, too, but that's not the reality of the game.

Montana and coach Bill Walsh were an ideally suited pair, even if they didn't always see eye to eye.

CHAPTER FIVE

1981:
A BREAKTHROUGH SEASON

he 49ers' outlook brightened gradually during Bill Walsh's first two seasons in San Francisco. When the team started 3-2 in 1981—the victories coming against lackluster teams—it looked as though the improvement would continue to be slow.

Then came a breakout game against the Dallas Cowboys. Dallas had tormented the 49ers in the early seventies, and had smoked the team 59-14 in 1980. In 1981, it was San Francisco that dizzied Dallas 45-14 at Candlestick Park. More big weekends followed, including back-to-back victories over the Rams and Steelers, teams that had faced off in the Super Bowl less than two years earlier.

The 49ers finished the regular season with the NFL's best record (13-3). Still, they were not the favorite to win it all. They had an unimpressive running game and a talented but inconsistent defense that featured three rookie starters in the secondary.

The 49ers again found Dallas in the way. In one of the most memorable games in NFL history, Joe Montana hit Dwight Clark at the back of the end zone with 51 seconds left on a play remembered simply as "The Catch," and San Francisco held on for a 28-27 win. Two weeks later, the 49ers won Super Bowl XVI, defeating Cincinnati 26-21. The ghosts of 35 years had been chased.

Fred Dean and Archie Reese jumped for joy when the 49ers claimed their first NFC championship.

KEITH FAHNHORST: I'm almost embarrassed to say it, but I was in my option year in '81. I was frustrated, and we started 1-2. To let you know how it was not yet obvious that we were turning things around, I asked John McVay to trade me. We were trying to get a contract done, and I thought, "Here we go again." So I sure as hell didn't see the thing turning around as quickly as it did....And, thank God, John McVay didn't listen to me. But I don't think we had the confidence and could see things were really improving until we beat Dallas by that big margin.

BILL MCPHERSON: The NFC Championship Game against the Cowboys here—I'm getting goose bumps just talking about it. I had coached in high school locally and at Santa Clara University....Now for us to be going to the Super Bowl for the first time, that was one of the great days. They replayed the game on (ESPN) Classic a couple months ago, and I got nervous all over again.

KEITH FAHNHORST: I'll never forget one play. Joe was rolling out. It was a naked bootleg, and (Dallas defensive end Ed) Too Tall Jones didn't really go for the fake, and came up the field. And Joe kind of ducked inside him and threw a long pass to Dwight. This was not The Catch. It was a touchdown to Dwight early in the game (to put San Francisco up

Lawrence Pillers, Paul Hofer, Archie Reese, and Dwaine Board appreciated Dwight Hicks' interception against Washington.

14-10). Well, the week before the game, Too Tall had made a couple comments about how he didn't know who the 49ers were, and didn't have a lot of respect for us, and that type of thing. And Joe turned to Too Tall after he threw that pass and he said, "Respect that, [expletive]." This young quarterback kind of got everybody fired up.

DWIGHT CLARK: I remember getting to the sideline after our touchdown with about a minute to go and realizing we still had to kick the extra point to win. I was coming off the field and looking up and seeing 27-27. And I don't think I realized (the score) until I actually saw it.

KEENA TURNER: Super Bowl XVI will always be etched in my memory because it was the first one, and also because I played and went through that game—and the NFC Championship—with some really extraordinary circumstances. I had chicken pox. The physical feelings I had always stand out. Being in Detroit, and feeling so sick, and wondering if I could play, and knowing there was no way I *wouldn't* play.

Center Fred Quillan reflected the 49ers' mood after a 17-14 victory at Pittsburgh improved their record to 7-2.

RANDY CROSS: One of the most lasting memories for me, Super Bowl-wise, was that first time. The day of the Super Bowl, getting to the stadium in Pontiac and walking out on that field with my buddy John Ayers, who was the other guard, and seeing what the place looked like. In the tunnel they're setting up to bring stuff out on the field. There's floats and things. It's just so different....I don't care how many times you see it on media day. That game-day look at that field, you're just, "Whoa, yes! This is why I always wanted to do this."

JOE MONTANA: You look at the first Super Bowl, when we played Cincinnati. My first memory is of that initial walk onto the field— hearing all the cheers and the boos. It was like a line that met at the 50-yard line. Half were cheers and half were boos when you walked onto the field.

EDDIE DEBARTOLO: I think the thing that turned that game around, believe it or not, was about a 20-yard sideline pass to Mike Wilson in the fourth quarter. It moved the chains. We were hav-

Coach Bill Walsh preceded the team to Pontiac, Michigan, for Super Bowl XVI, and greeted his players disguised as a bell captain.

ing some trouble with Cincinnati. Strange as it may seem, that's the play that sticks out in my mind, other than the goal-line stand and Danny Bunz's hit on (Charles) Alexander.

JOHN MCVAY: We had an offensive lineman (John Choma) who played on our defensive line in goal-line situations. And (the Bengals) ran a sucker. They ran a play where the right guard pulls. If you have a defensive lineman who knows what to do, he's following the guard. Well, they ran that play and handed off to the fullback. But (Choma) didn't know what to do. He just stayed there and made the tackle. People probably thought, "Man did they play that perfectly!" But what the hell.

BILL MCPHERSON: The Eagles went to Super Bowl XV (and lost to Oakland) in 1980, and (long-time friend and coach Dick) Vermeil called me and said, "Well, how do you feel about that? We've got a Super Bowl ring and a Super Bowl check."

So then we went to the Super Bowl the next year, and I called Dick back. I said, "Dick, I'm gonna show you what a first-place ring looks like and (what) a first-place check looks like."

After Dwight Clark (87) came down with "The Catch" against the Cowboys, the 49ers earned their first of five Super Bowl trips.

CHAPTER SIX

THE WEST COAST OFFENSE

he offensive system that Bill Walsh developed in San Francisco did not spring from his mind spontaneously. He picked up elements from NFL coaching legends Sid Gillman, Paul Brown, and Don Coryell, and he spent a good deal of time honing the scheme through trial and error. Whatever the origins, Walsh's offenses staggered NFL defenses for a decade and beyond with their presnap motion, short drops, "hot" reads, and carefully detailed passing progression.

Some of the 49ers' innovations—such as the 25-play offensive "script" Walsh used to begin each game—were widely reported. Others—such as Bobb McKittrick's complex blocking schemes—were noticed only by insiders. Most of them have been copied in the intervening years. The 49ers still run a version of the West Coast offense, as it was dubbed, as do three quarters of the NFL's other teams.

But Walsh's system was not limited to the offensive playbook. He instituted methods of training, practicing, and scouting that were equally responsible for San Francisco's long run of success.

The West Coast offense wasn't just about passing, as Roger Craig demonstrated against the Washington Redskins.

BILL WALSH: I think we started in Cincinnati with it, with our football, so to speak. I took (the ideas) to San Diego (in 1976) and had a chance to install and implement it there and teach all its nuances with Dan Fouts and Charlie Joiner and others. Then I went to Stanford and did the exact same thing. The Stanford players, to be honest with you, could pick up the offense quicker than the pros. In fact, it was more sophisticated at Stanford. Then when I went to the 49ers, I had another opportunity to install it.

So I had become really at ease with installing and developing the offense, and developing a way of teaching it, and the drills to teach it, and the strategy and everything....By then it had become a true system of football. We didn't label it. It was just the way we played....And what we did was liberally use the forward pass on early downs, first down in particular, and have a comprehensive base of offensive football, from the run to the pass, to depend equally on both, without being predictable.

JOE MONTANA: All we were trying to do was keep constant pressure on the defense. If you gain four or five yards, next thing you know, you're 30 yards down field after five or six plays, and the defense is thinking "Dang, they've only completed four- or five-yard passes." The defense wins the bat-

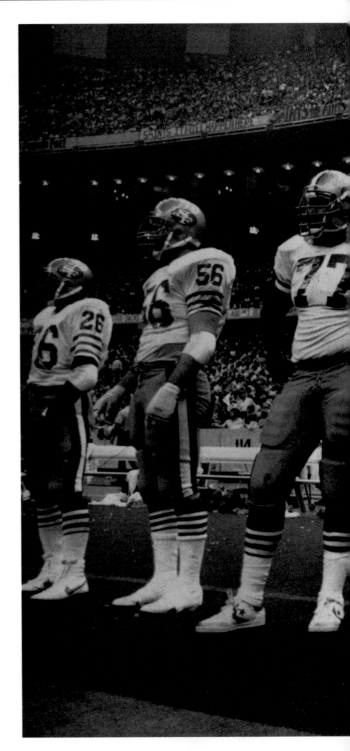

The play of the offensive linemen—Fred Quillan (56), Bubba Paris (77), Keith Fahnhorst (71), Randy Cross (51), John Ayers (68)— was fundamental to the success of the system.

tle, but loses the war. That's what that system is about.

ROGER CRAIG: Understanding those three reads, that's so important....It stuck in my head: one-two-three, you know? You read the primary, the first receiver. If this guy's covered, you go to your secondary receiver. If he's covered, you dump off to Roger or you dump off to Wendell Tyler or you dump off to Tom Rathman. Those are the things the quarterback has to be able to do *quickly*. I mean, it has to be precise.

We liked for defenses to blitz us. We loved it. Most teams worried, "How are we gonna handle this blitz?" Not us. We knew how to pick up blitzes. We knew who the hot receivers were.

BILL WALSH: We were, along with the Dallas Cowboys, really the only teams in football using the man in motion. And we developed the tight end in motion, which is very popular now.

ROGER CRAIG: We'd just run a lot of different formations. We had trips (three-wide-receiver) formations, we had formations with just one back in the backfield, or two backs with me and Wendell Tyler—and then Tom Rathman a little later. One back would stay and block, the other would go out. My favorite play was called "Bingo Cross." Both of the halfbacks are crossing, starting about five yards apart from each other.

GUY MCINTYRE: We ran a lot of pulls, a lot of traps, and a lot of sweeps. And it was demanding. Our scheme of picking up blitzes and stunts, and just recognizing defenses, all had to be on cue. It demanded a lot from us, and it demanded a lot of communication along the line.

But it was also fun. I mean, we were kind of notorious as a finesse team. But then a lot of people complained about us cut blocking people....I think the 49ers were one of the least-liked offensive lines in the league for a long time

It was a fun offensive line because I got to use my athletic ability pulling on sweeps, running down the field in front of running backs. That got you notoriety, more so than if you just stayed in there and pounded the ball downfield, three yards and a cloud of dust.

ROGER CRAIG: We weren't an overpowering running team. But we'd run quick traps, on-the-edge type plays, hitting them on the edge, and just throwing the defense off track a bit.

Play-action faking was big in our system, too. Joe Montana and I used to work on play-action faking all the time....If I gave a good fake and pulled the safety up, Jerry Rice and John Taylor were gonna be wide open. They would be one-on-one with those guys. And they were gonna win.

GUY MCINTYRE: You knew where you had to go, and you had to be able to block in space, and you had to be able to make a double-team block and release

By the time Bill Walsh brought the West Coast offense to San Francisco, he was an old hand at explaining its intricacies.

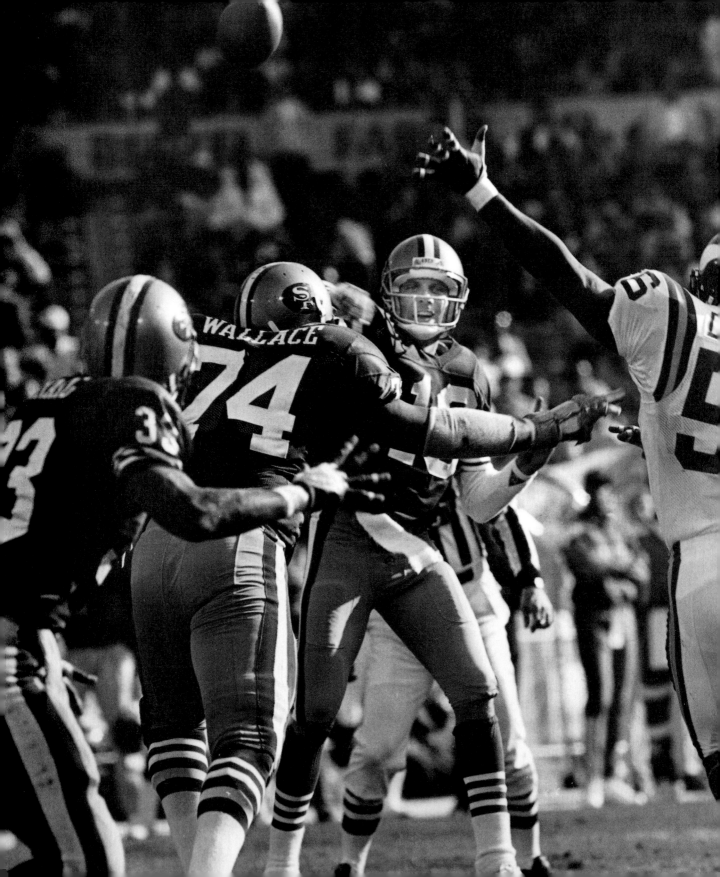

and get to the linebacker. If you blocked one guy, you might double-team the down lineman and then you had to watch and see which side the linebacker comes off, depending on whether you were gonna release and get the next man or whether you were double-teaming with the tackle, guard, or center.

With Joe Montana in the backfield, pass protection was a challenge. Because you knew that if you gave him the opportunity, he would wait to get the ball to the right person.

ROGER CRAIG: In training camp we never really worked that hard. We worked more in the classroom than we did on the football field. Even in Super Bowl XXIV, the Denver Broncos were beating themselves up doing two-a-days, and we met (indoors) most of the time. We went out there fresh and ready to go. I think training camp's overrated. A lot of teams like to beat themselves up. Bill Walsh took the opposite approach. His thing was, "Let's understand the system."

GUY MCINTYRE: I went to Green Bay (in 1994), and Mike Holmgren was there at the time. He had just come from San Francisco. And then I went to

Everything clicked against the Cowboys in 1985 when Dwight Clark and Roger Craig enjoyed a 31-16 victory.

Philadelphia (in 1995), and Ray Rhodes was there with Jon Gruden. So even though I went to different teams, they still implemented the same type of offense, a lot of the same pickup schemes.

BILL MCPHERSON: We're still in the same program, and people are using his offense with other teams. For example, my son works for the Denver Broncos. And I know exactly where he's gonna be during the day because their schedule for coaches and players and meetings and practice and walk-throughs is exactly what was established here years ago (when Mike) Shanahan was (an assistant coach) here.

MIKE WALTER: We had some phenomenal defensive years. But the truth is, you ask any of those guys who played defense, we couldn't wait to get off the field so we could watch the offense. Our deal was, "Let's get our three downs and get out, and let's watch these guys go to work." Because it was something else to watch those guys—to watch Joe Montana, and to watch Jerry Rice, and to watch Freddie Solomon and Dwight Clark and Roger Craig. That was like poetry out there.

Joe Montana had a remarkable faculty for reading pass coverages, scanning the field, and locating a receiver.

CHAPTER SEVEN

ALL IN THE FAMILY

hough they know it reeks of cliché, veterans of the 49ers' glory years often describe the team as a family. This was, indeed, an extremely close-knit group away from the field, too. Much of the camaraderie extended from Eddie DeBartolo and the fidelity (and material reward) he showed to those in the fold. Some of it derived from the era began before free agency redefined the NFL—a time when most players expected to play for one team throughout their careers.

The 49ers continued to excel through the mid-1990s, but the familial feeling began to dissipate as the salary cap forced a revolving door of personnel. For better or worse, the days of team-as-family might be gone for good.

Teammates mobbed Ray Wersching in week 14 of the 1980 season after his overtime field goal defeated New Orleans.

EDDIE DeBARTOLO: I have spent hours—and I mean hours and hours—talking to Joe, Ronnie, Freddie Solomon, Keith Fahnhorst. I could go on and on. I have spent hours with these guys, over dinner, over wine, over beer, over nothing. Hot dogs. This could not be done again. I mean, we were friends. I mean, when a guy went down it was like one of my kids was hurt....

Did some owners try to duplicate what I did, and what Bill did? Yes, of course they did. But you can't just say to John Doe, "You know, I'm going to get close to you and I'm gonna be your friend." It just came natural for us because that's the way my father ran our company. At one point we had 13,000 employees. We must have had close to 700 people in our Youngstown, Ohio, office (at DeBartolo corporate headquarters). And every single one of them felt as though they were part of our family. I just carried that on to the 49ers.

BILL WALSH: We would have gatherings each year that Ed DeBartolo would obviously underwrite, for our whole staff and their wives. Everybody was included. We'd open the wine, and everybody in the room was expected to give a toast—women, men, everybody. It was really fun. We just had a wonderful time early on because we were all naïve and so excited and euphoric about our success.

The San Francisco 49ers, young and old, were all members of one big happy family during the dynasty years.

Owner Eddie DeBartolo was as much a member of the team as any of the players in cleats and pads.

EDDIE DeBARTOLO: We did things that were different. We had parties with the families at Christmas, with Santa Clauses. You know, we'd have a black Santa Claus and a white Santa Claus. We did things during the year. We had cookouts for the wives at Christmastime. I'd send roses to the mothers and the wives. It was just different.

RANDY CROSS: I'm not sure if any team in the history of the NFL ever had as much fun as the '81 team did. I mean, we had more fun than allowed by law in a lot of states. We had a great time— which showed the next year in '82 (when the 49ers finished 3-6 in a strike-shortened season)....It was a close

The players shared a bond on and off the field, even when it came to a friendly hand of poker en route to the next game.

team. We partied together, we ate together, we drank together, we watched *Monday Night Football* together. As the years wore on and guys got married and had families and what-not, there was less and less of that.

JESSE SAPOLU: We still have the record of winning 18 straight road games in a span of almost 2½ years (1988-1990). When we got away from home, it was almost like we were getting away from the dis-

tractions of our own families. That's how focused those teams were. We couldn't wait to get away from home because we realized that when we played at home, our minds were on making sure that we entertained guests, and making sure our wives were taking care of our families. When we went on the road it was just a team in a hotel. We would step on the football field during warm-ups, in front of a lot of hostile crowds, and have that aura about us that we were seven points ahead already.

RANDY CROSS: There was "Us" and there was "Them." The hard part about Us is that Us is basically the team, the coaches, the organization at that time. I mean, from a week-to-week basis. If you're hurt, you're not Us. If you were released two days ago, you're not Us. If you retired a day ago, you're still not Us. You're treated very well, but you're still not part of the Us-and-Them deal.

MATT MILLEN: Eddie DeBartolo flew our families to Hawaii—the whole team—for our ring ceremonies (in 1990). We spent time together, and got to enjoy being together, away from football, away from practices, in the offseason, where we could just sit and talk to each other and rehash things in a relaxed atmosphere. And that was just a wonderful experience.

JOE MONTANA: I hear myself saying the things I hear some of the older players who played before me say. And I'm like, "Okay, I've gotta stop that...." But free agency had a huge impact on teams keeping players together.

JESSE SAPOLU: I played long enough to last into free agency, and that revolving door was something I didn't like. We started losing Guy McIntyre, who went to Green Bay and Philadelphia. Joe went to Kansas City, Ronnie went to the Raiders, Roger Craig went to the Raiders.

I was with the 49ers when I saw these guys—who I went to war with, who understood what the standard was because of the system and the way it was set up—start going somewhere else. I missed the old way when we were close, and stayed together for 10 or 11 years. We didn't like players from other teams, we didn't socialize with them too much off the field. Nowadays, it's almost like if you have the same agent as a player from another team, you're closer to that player than you are to your own teammates.

Even after a loss to the Chicago Bears in 1988, the 49ers united in the locker room for a moment of reflection.

CHAPTER EIGHT

THE EMOTIONAL LEADER

he archetypal anecdote about Ronnie Lott recounts the time, late in the 1985 season, when doctors recommended surgery to repair the tip of his left pinky finger. The 49ers' star defensive back didn't want to miss any playing time in recuperation, so he chose a simpler procedure. He had the finger amputated above the third knuckle. He didn't miss a down.

Many less dramatic stories establish Lott as the 49ers' emotional leader. He knocked himself out—and knocked out a few opponents, too— for the team, and he didn't hesitate to upbraid teammates who were inclined to give anything less than 100 percent.

Lott was quite a player, too. He still holds the 49ers' record with 51 career interceptions. He played in four Pro Bowls as a cornerback before making the switch to safety. It was an astute move. It kept Lott at his peak even after he lost a half step of speed later in his career, and it capitalized on the trait that eventually made him legendary: his pad-popping hits.

Ronnie Lott played with a ferocity that was impossible to ignore.

ERIC WRIGHT: When guys did not do their job, they got jumped. That's what kept us a disciplined group. A lot of times we would fight on the field and argue among ourselves just because guys weren't doing their jobs, and we would correct it on the field. It could come from anyone, but Ronnie basically could police that. You know what? You would hate the guy on the field, but then again, you respected him because he made plays. If he wasn't making plays and he was still moaning and bitching, no one would respect him. But he could back it up.

MIKE WALTER: There's some history with Ronnie and me—and Ronnie and a lot of different guys. When I was new, in those first few years, I think

whenever someone ran up the middle, it didn't make any difference whose gap it went through, Ronnie came looking for me. Because in Ronnie's mind, it probably came from my hole. You had to kind of earn respect from Ronnie. I can remember one time in the huddle, having to pull him and Keena Turner away from each other. They were ready to go at it.

KEENA TURNER: Were there confrontations? Hell, yeah. But they were miniscule in terms of the level of the relationships involved, and what was attained. Ronnie pushed. He pushed himself and he pushed all of us, and he demanded it. He demanded a certain kind of perfection that we all learned to appreciate and to demand of ourselves.

HARRIS BARTON: If we won championships and Joe Montana's not the quarterback, Ronnie Lott's the MVP of three or four games. He had a presence in the locker room. No one ever screwed around in practice. Ronnie was serious. He was a team guy, a loyal guy. A guy would give up a touch- down, and Ronnie would be the first guy over there to pat him on the back and say, "Hey, let's get going." But he'd also be the first guy over there to tell him how to correct himself.

ROGER CRAIG: You know how the lion is the king of the jungle? Ronnie Lott, in my eyes, was like that. He was like the king of football....He'd do whatever

Neither teammates nor opponents had difficulty reading Lott's emotions.

it takes to win. I judge a leader by how a guy plays and how he works. Ronnie Lott was all that. And then he was a team spokesman. He would even voice his opinion to coaches, management, whatever. He stuck his neck out for a lot of his teammates. That shows the character of a great leader, and a warrior. He was a true, true warrior. Just getting the tip of his finger cut off and coming back to play, that shows what kind of guy he was.

MIKE WALTER: When it came down to the very end of a game and you needed a play, he could make it. And I don't know how he did it. He'd come up with the interception, he'd come up with the big hit for a fumble. Maybe Joe Montana had that same kind of ability. But I never had that ability. Very few guys ever do. I never had that ability to step up and make a huge play when you needed to. I mean, I'd like to say I did. But I didn't. And most guys don't. Ninety-nine percent of the guys who played don't have that....But Ronnie had that ability like no one I ever played with, and it didn't matter how he played the whole game. When it came down to the last play, if you needed to make a play, he came up with it somehow. Even to this day it still floors me.

ROGER CRAIG: He was the only one to keep (volatile pass rusher) Charles Haley in line. It's

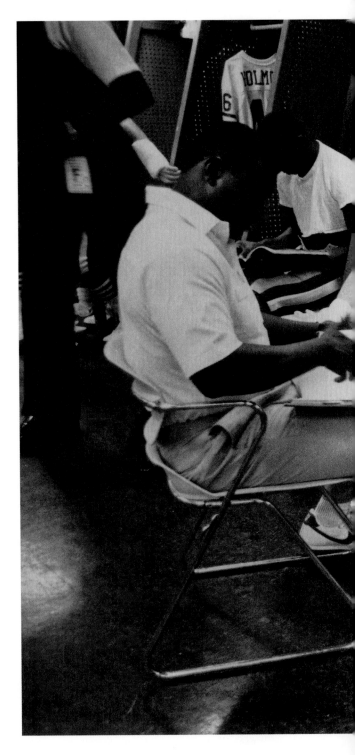

Lott (flanked by Tom Holmoe and Jeff Fuller) was a bundle of energy on game day, as he demonstrated during a 1984 pregame session with assistant coach Ray Rhodes.

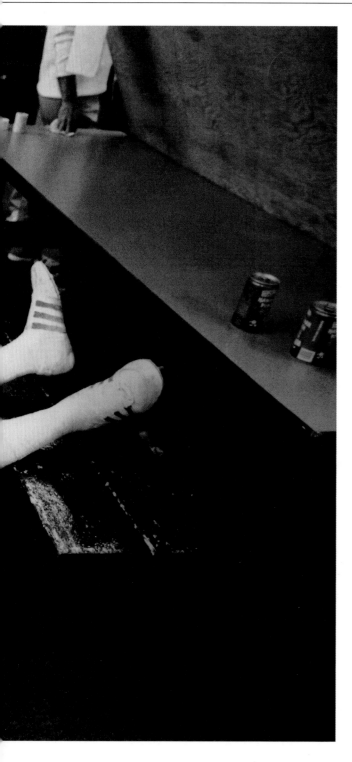

amazing. I remember later in our careers Ronnie and I were (playing for) the Raiders, and Charles Haley was having a fit in the San Francisco locker room because we'd beat the 49ers. They had to come into the Raiders' locker room to get Ronnie to go calm Charles down.

RONNIE LOTT: I think that when I played at USC, I had the good fortune of...having a great coach by the name of John Robinson, who said, "When you go out there, you try to get respect from your opponent."

And that's the ultimate compliment. Even if you lose the game, if your opponent respects you, that's more important. When I got to the 49ers, that was important to me, that every time I walked out there I was trying to get respect from my opponents, from my teammates, from my peers. And it got to the point where you wanted to have that from everyone—your fans, the people you came in contact with. Because at the end of the day, that's all you have.

ROGER CRAIG: He's a very intense person. I had a marketing company with him. And he had the same kind of attitude in marketing.

The man of action relaxed during halftime of a 1986 victory over the Rams, in which he made his tenth interception of the season.

CHAPTER NINE

1984:
A TEAM WITHOUT
A WEAKNESS

fter an embarrassing collapse in 1982 and a near (and controversial) miss in 1983, the 49ers rolled to the Super Bowl again in 1984.

Unlike the '81 team, which relied heavily on the magic of Joe Montana and the mystifying play calling of Bill Walsh, the '84 squad was solid on every front. Wendell Tyler and Roger Craig, both acquired a year earlier, jelled in the backfield. A number of trades—especially those for defensive tackles Manu Tuiasosopo and Gary Johnson—cemented the defense.

The 49ers lost only one game, by 3 points to Pittsburgh, and marched resolutely through the postseason.

A 23-0 shutout of Chicago in the NFC Championship Game earned the 49ers a trip to nearby Stanford Stadium for Super Bowl XIX—meaning that they owned the next-best thing to a home-field advantage. San Francisco beat the high-powered Dolphins—and their second-year sensation of a quarterback, Dan Marino—by the convincing margin of 38-16.

The specter of Dan Marino loomed over Super Bowl XIX as the 49ers waited to be introduced.

ROGER CRAIG: We knew we were so close in '83, my rookie year, to being in the Super Bowl. The Washington Redskins lucked out with two phantom calls against our defensive backs. We were called for pass interference (in the NFC title game), but we couldn't find it anywhere (on film).

But instead of us going into the tank, we said, "Okay, next year is gonna be our year. We're coming back with a vengeance." So the guys were focused, and we played hard all year long. We had one messup. Pittsburgh beat us (in week 7), and that kind of humbled us a bit to get on track.

RONNIE LOTT: It was the most talented team that I'd ever been around. There were people on that team who had been all-pros. There were people on that team who were becoming all-pros....And the intensity and the energy of that group grew every week. (We) had people who wouldn't accept anything but winning. And that year, more so than any other year, we just exuded talent.

KEITH FAHNHORST: That was a whole different set of pressures we had to deal with because we were favored by a lot of people to play really well that year. So there was that added pressure.

As the clock ticked down before kickoff at Super Bowl XIX, coach Bill Walsh and a locker room full of players counted the minutes and tried to find a way to relax.

DWIGHT HICKS: We had Fred Dean, Dwaine Board, Manu Tuiasosopo, Michael Carter, and Lawrence Pillers on the defensive line. I remember them being very stellar in putting a good pass rush on quarterbacks. They just told us, "Give us a few seconds, and we'll get our jobs done." So even though we took it upon our shoulders as a secondary (all four starters at cornerback and safety made the Pro Bowl), it was a collective unit and a collective effort.

The Bears had a really good season. They were coming along as a power in the NFL....Our defense just took it upon itself (in the NFC Championship Game) to say, "Hey, let's step it up. Get a lot of numbers [tacklers] to Walter Payton, who's a great running back, and we'll be successful." We did so.

BILL MCPHERSON: When we played Miami at Stanford in the Super Bowl, we had probably the best defensive team we had here. My old defensive line coach at Santa Clara (Mike Scarry) was the defensive line coach for the Dolphins. Plus, (former 49ers defensive coordinator Chuck) Studley was on that staff at that time. For a guy like Walsh or me, local guys for a long time, we're playing the Super Bowl right in our back yard. I mean, all your relatives, all your friends. It cost me a fortune because all these people needed Super Bowl tickets.

KEITH FAHNHORST: Marino had had just a fantastic year (setting NFL records with 5,084 passing yards and 48 touchdowns). And I think a lot of people started almost disregarding us, or taking us for granted by the time we got to the Super Bowl. I know Joe Montana took it personally that Marino was getting so much attention.

Wendell Tyler (left) and Roger Craig provided the 1984 49ers with a potent running attack.

The players gathered in the shower room for a silent prayer before taking the field against the Miami Dolphins.

ROGER CRAIG: I can remember right before the Super Bowl everybody was talking about Miami, how hot Dan Marino was. They were supposed to blow us away. So our defense wanted to prove something to them. And our offense really took it personally. We really wanted to show them up. It was probably the most intense game I've ever played in my career.

BILL MCPHERSON: The night before the game, (*Sports Illustrated* writer) Paul Zimmerman sees me in the lobby of the hotel. I'm going to a meeting. He says, "Mac, how can you expect to get to Marino? He gets rid of the ball in like 1.6 seconds or something."

I said, "God, I wish you hadn't told me that. Now you've really got me worried."

But we had some really good rushers in Dwaine Board and Fred Dean. We had a great scheme.

JOE MONTANA: In '84, we're playing at home, basically, at Stanford. When the fog rolled over

Owner Eddie DeBartolo wore the look of a winner as he congratulated Super Bowl XIX MVP Joe Montana.

the edge of the stadium, it was typical weather for us. The perfect setting for us to win. It's our weather, it's our place, it's our home field.

BILL WALSH: I think the greatest game (Montana) played, of all games, was Super Bowl XIX against Miami. He played a perfect game. If I hadn't held him back, we'd have scored more touchdowns. And we were playing a team that had lost only two games. Miami was 14-2 that year.

MICHAEL ZAGARIS: When we won the Super Bowl, I remember we took a bus back to the team hotel, and we went over El Camino Real, where cars are like bumper to bumper and everyone's honking. And it was as if we were sort of outside of ourselves, like everybody's going crazy and we're in the middle of this. We got back to our hotel, and everybody got in their cars and went to some private parties. But there was no big celebration.

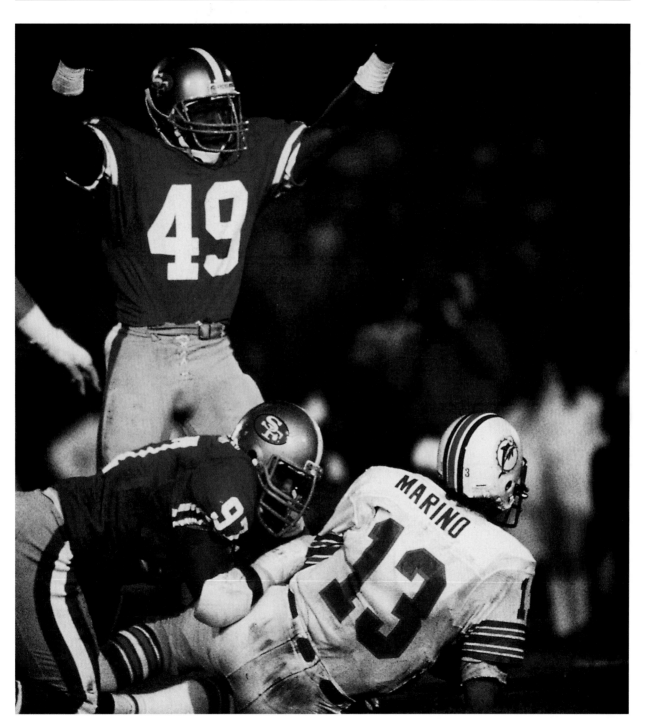

Safety Jeff Fuller (49) and defensive tackle Gary Johnson had reason to celebrate a sack of Dan Marino.

CHAPTER TEN

SUPERSTAR STAFF

he list of assistant coaches who worked under Bill Walsh and George Seifert reads like a Who's Who of NFL brainpower from the last two decades. Pete Carroll, Bruce Coslet, Jeff Fisher, Dennis Green, Mike Holmgren, Ray Rhodes, Mike Shanahan, Mike White, Sam Wyche—they all roamed the sidelines at Candlestick Park before acquiring NFL head-coaching positions elsewhere. When you consider third-generation spin-offs such as Andy Reid,

Jon Gruden, and Steve Mariucci, all of whom studied under Holmgren, the net is cast even wider.

It's hard to say whether the 49ers were better at finding talented young coaches, or teaching them the game once they got to San Francisco. Certainly, both occurred. But there is no doubt that the 49ers' intelligent group of assistants was a big reason for the team's success. It also represents continuing proof of Walsh's league-wide legacy.

Long before Mike Holmgren won acclaim as a head coach, he earned his spurs as Joe Montana's position coach.

RANDY CROSS: We knew we had a great staff because other teams kept trying to hire our people. Year after year after year, we were losing offensive and defensive coaches....We had those kinds of coaches. And the family tree reads like something out of that section of the Bible that's always "begetting." You know, Bill begat Mike, and Mike begat the other Mike, and the other Mike begat Andy. It goes on and on.

BILL WALSH: Basically, the reason so many of our men and their protégés have gone on—like Mike Holmgren and all the men who have left him—is the style of management and the requirement that everybody participate in the process. So there weren't people left out of the process of making decisions—making trades, selecting players, strategizing. Everyone was expected to be a party to it. To be honest, I may have approached it that way myself regardless, but I did learn to do that both when I was with Al Davis and when I was with Paul Brown.

MIKE WALTER: Dallas (where he played in 1983) was a very top-down organization. Tom Landry told the assistant coaches what to do, and the assistant coaches told the players. And none of the information went the other way.

All of a sudden, I got to the 49ers, and we'd have these meetings, and Coach Walsh would let the other coaches do things. The coaches would say in the meeting, "Hey, we could do it this way or we could do it that way. What would be the best way to do it?" Which was totally foreign to me after coming from Dallas, where Coach Landry ran the projector for both the offense and the defense after a game, and no one else said a thing.

BILL WALSH: I think a lot of it was the ability to communicate, and being consumed with the game of football and strategies and tactics. Being real technicians who could communicate. And, of course, all the other tangibles like work ethic. We had people who communicated well, who had a lot of energy, and who really thrived on offensive and defensive football.

JOE MONTANA: I had a fairly good rapport, I think, with all the guys I worked with directly, those who coached the quarterback position especially— from Sam Wyche to Paul Hackett to Mike Holmgren. I didn't have much time with Mike Shanahan. But those first three guys arrived at the right times in my career.

Sam really hung on and just beat basics into my brain—footwork and reading defenses, typical stuff a quarterback needs to know to be able to perform on a day-to-day basis. Paul Hackett, on the other hand, expanded the idea of perfection. I mean, he did not like us to fail on one play....Paul came around after I had some time under my belt and just said, "Okay, this is it. Your footwork needs to be this way, it needs to be perfect. Why'd you throw the ball there when this guy's open? What did you see?"...

In 1980, Sam Wyche counseled Steve DeBerg (who needed a voice-amplification system to call signals because of laryngitis).

And Mike Holmgren: "Gotta put the ball in the air, and we're gonna have fun." He expanded the offense and let you be a little bit freer.

HARRIS BARTON: The one thing that Mike (Shanahan) does better than anybody, in my opinion, is halftime adjustments....In the 1994 season (when Shannahan was offensive coordinator), he was just amazing the way he could adjust. Teams traditionally played the 49ers very differently than

they had their other opponents.

You'd look at film all week long of a team—say the Atlanta Falcons—and they'd run a certain type of defense. You know, you could watch seven games of film on them, and in six games they'd run a similar type of defense, and in the seventh game something that was a variation. But then you'd come in and play 'em, and they'd come out with something just totally, radically different. It was so radical, there was no way you could prepare for it during the

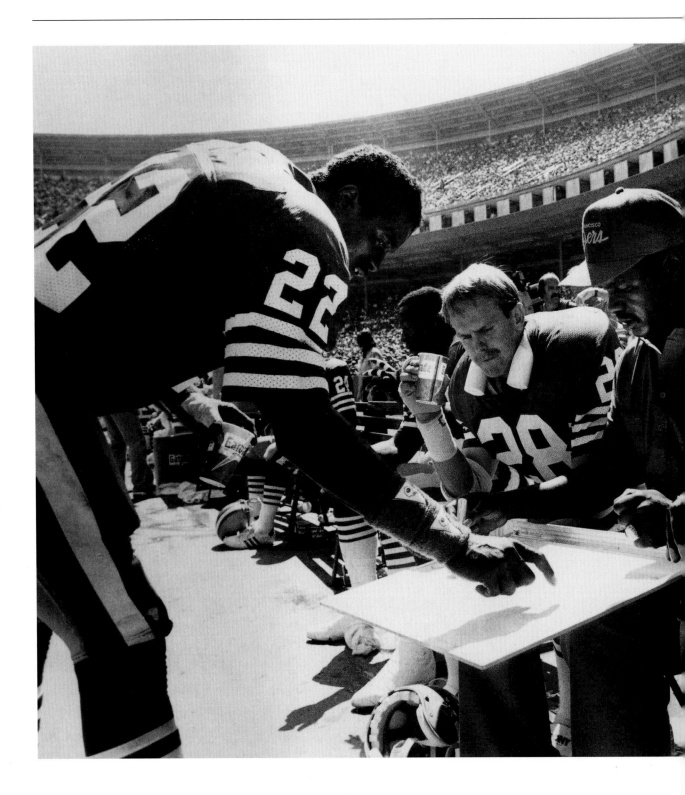

week. What it took was an offensive mind that could adjust the game plan to fit the defense we were playing. Mike did that better than anybody.

MIKE WALTER: (Bill McPherson) was a huge influence on the defensive side of the ball—especially for the defensive linemen and linebackers. He was the kind of guy you wanted to play hard for. He's still around today. He's almost your father-type figure out there. He's gonna be really hard on you. He's gonna tell you how it really is. But at the end of it all, if you gave it your best, he's gonna appreciate you and love you for what you did.

BILL McPHERSON: I think there have been two, maybe three, coaches fired here in 23 years. Hell, that's unheard of.

Ray Rhodes, then defensive backs coach, conferred with Dwight Hicks (22), Tom Holmoe (28), and Carlton Williamson in 1984.

CHAPTER ELEVEN

THE DEFENSE
NEVER RESTED

Maybe it was the 49ers' reputation as a "finesse" team. Maybe it was simply the long shadow cast by Bill Walsh's offense. But the San Francisco defense rarely got the accolades the players—offensive and defensive—felt it deserved.

In Walsh's first two seasons, the defense was generally porous. But after that it remained solid throughout the dynasty. The 49ers ranked in the NFL's top six (in fewest total yards allowed) seven times, leading the league in 1987 and finishing second in 1981. Thirteen different defensive players earned a total of 32 Pro Bowl selections from 1981-1994.

The mastermind of the scheme was George Seifert, an early promoter of situational substitution. Seifert arrived to coach defensive backs in 1980, and three years later was promoted to defensive coordinator. When he became head coach in 1989, he retained oversight of the defense.

On his fishing excursions out of Bodega Bay, Seifert could be laid back and funny. But when it came to football he was frightfully intense, almost absurdly detail oriented. Six years after leaving the 49ers, Seifert's reputation, as a blackboard whiz and a true character, remains intact.

Though overshadowed by their offensive mates, the 49ers could play defense, as John Elway discovered in Super Bowl XXIV.

BILL McPHERSON: When we were able to acquire (middle linebacker) Hacksaw Reynolds and (end) Fred Dean for our defensive group, then draft Ronnie Lott and Eric Wright (all in 1981), then we had something going.

Hacksaw taught the younger players how to study. Fred Dean taught the linemen how to rush the passer, how to work hard. Those guys helped us get this thing going faster than we expected. We (had already) brought in Dwight Hicks to be our (free) safety. Dwight was working in a health food store in Detroit (when the 49ers signed him in 1979).... Dwight was really a smart guy from the University of Michigan. He came in and he was like the coach of those guys back there, in terms of being a steadying influence on the young players.

KEENA TURNER: We won Super Bowl XVI with Chuck Studley as defensive coordinator with a very simple defense. We did very, very few things. And it was probably the best thing for us, because we were a young team.

RONNIE LOTT: You combine a new defensive scheme, along with the three rookies (in the secondary), along with bringing in Hacksaw Reynolds and Fred Dean, and there wasn't a lot you could do in terms of trying to experiment.

The defense evolved from a very conservative defense, a defense that played (primarily) a cover-3 (zone), and a defense that just made sure that we didn't give up the big play, to a defense (by the late 1980s) that became a very attacking defense, a defense that wanted to do a variety of different things. That tone was set by George Seifert.

ERIC WRIGHT: George taught us that you have to know about the Xs and Os side of the business. As a group of young guys, we didn't always understand why he was drilling us so hard, making us spend a lot of time. We'd be the first guys into meetings and the last ones out of meetings. But it paid off because we knew a lot about the scheme....You don't get beat by physical talent when you get to this level. You get beat by neglecting the details, guys not doing their jobs. And George was a real stickler for that.

RONNIE LOTT: I go back to 1981, when George had all of us as young pups, rookies. That year, he would drill us and drill us and drill us after every practice. It was kind of funny. Joe Montana and others would stick their heads in and say, "You can let 'em go home now."

There were more than a few times in those meetings after practice when George would ask you certain questions, and if you didn't answer appropriately, he would keep you in there. There were a number of times that there were some guys, including me, who would want George to take it easy because the afternoons were growing fairly long. But looking back on it, had he not done that, I don't think we would have been able to accelerate our skills the way we did.

The addition of studious linebacker Jack (Hacksaw) Reynolds helped solidify the defense in 1981.

ERIC WRIGHT: George is a real standoffish guy. Even though he was our position coach, he never really got close to the secondary. It seemed like it was all business. To get to know George, you had to catch him out hunting or fishing. Then it's a totally different story. Even today, you have to put George in his environment for him to open up.

KEENA TURNER: Much like Bill, George was consumed with the idea that you could stop everything, that you could come up with a defensive response to everything, that there was a check you could make, that there was an adjustment that had to happen.

We used to have days we called "What If" days. George would come in on a Friday and just throw bizarre plays at us. You've already prepared for what you're going to do, and now it's What If day. That means anything could happen on the football field. Could our defense respond to it and adjust to it? The evolution was that we *were* ready for everything, we *did* respond to everything. And it meant our list of defenses just grew and grew and grew.

RONNIE LOTT: The strength of George's defenses was that we could change. For example, the flexibility of having (linebacker) Keena Turner—you could play him over the tight end and he could take a tight end one-on-one almost like a strong safety—to having Charles Haley, who could play a defensive

George Seifert was a taskmaster on defense, consumed with the idea that any opponent could be stopped in its tracks.

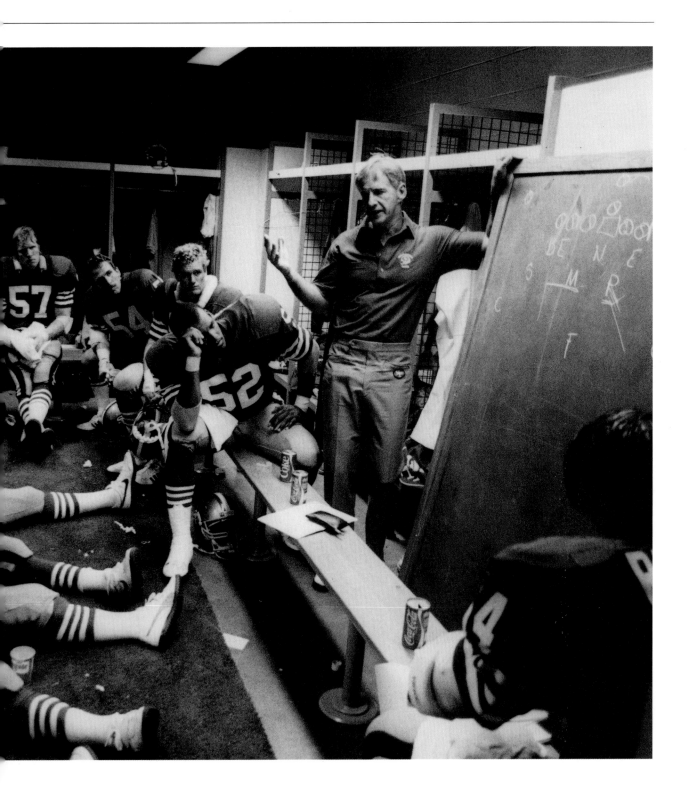

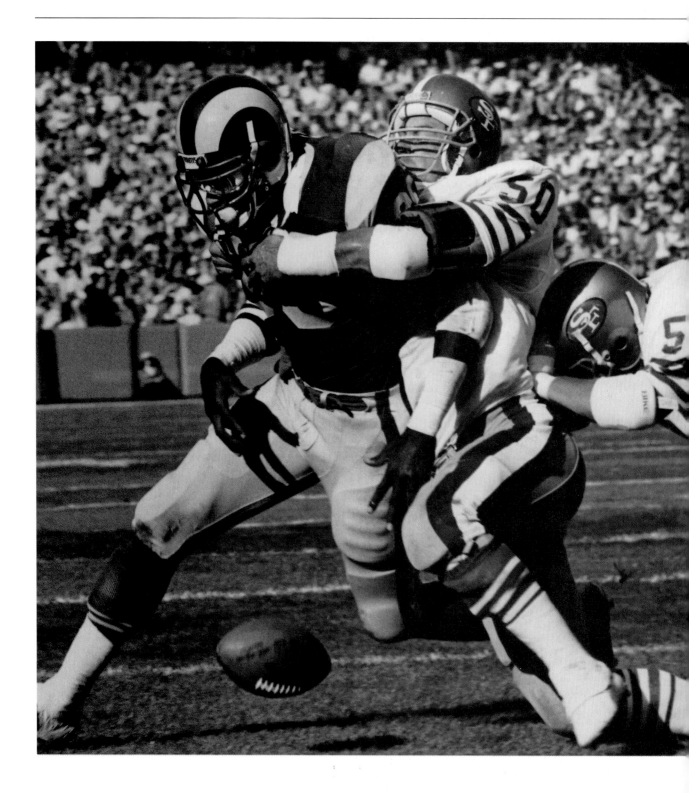

end or middle linebacker, roving around the field from that position....We brought in Michael Carter and Big Hands (Johnson) and Louie Kelcher (in 1984), and put those three guys over the center-guard-tackle when we played Dan Marino and (the Dolphins) in Super Bowl XIX. George did an excellent job of constantly trying to put players in positions where they could use their ability—but more important, to put players in positions where *he* could scheme to make it difficult on the offense.

KEENA TURNER: To be honest with you, by the end of my career I wondered: Would I have been able to come into this defense as a veteran and keep up, without having had the opportunity to learn the nuances of it as I had done?

Linebackers Riki Ellison and Milt McColl found the best way to stop Eric Dickerson was to separate him from the ball.

CHAPTER TWELVE

UPHOLDING
THE STANDARD

rom Gary (Big Hands) Johnson to Matt Millen to Charles Mann, the 49ers had an uncanny knack for bringing in aging players, plugging them into the scheme, and coaxing a productive year or two out of them.

One of the reasons was the eye for talent first demonstrated by Bill Walsh and augmented by seasoned scouts such as Tony Razzano. But just as important, newcomers tended to find a higher gear when they came to San Francisco. They responded to the classy treatment they received and to the work ethic exhibited by an important core of 49ers. Players such as Jack (Hacksaw) Reynolds and Ronnie Lott demanded fanaticism on the field, while Roger Craig and Jerry Rice led by example, pushing their practice habits and offseason workouts to a new level of suffering.

It all added up to an unmistakable mystique. Anyone joining the 49ers knew he'd have to work harder than ever, but the rewards could be substantial.

The example set by superstars such as Joe Montana and Jerry Rice, helped motivate newcomers to the 49ers.

RANDY CROSS: The reason that football team stayed successful for so long was the foundation— the organization behind it—which was the greatest thing Bill Walsh ever built. He laid the groundwork for the way the 49ers did business. Because you plugged people in, and it didn't matter if it was Hacksaw Reynolds or Fred Dean or Tim Harris or Wendell Tyler or Deion Sanders. When you came into that organization, everyone around you let you know pretty quickly what was expected of you. There was no gray area.

JESSE SAPOLU: A new player would be able to tell just from the speed of practices....I remember jumping offside as a rookie, and I kind of knew already that was a serious offense during our practices. And all of a sudden I heard a voice saying, "Mr. Jesse Sapolu, where do you think you're at? This is not Hawaii." I was kind of embarrassed.

ROGER CRAIG: They didn't give me a year to get ready (as a rookie in 1983). I had to get ready in three or four weeks. I had to be ready to go, because I was a starter at fullback. I had to play at a championship level because they'd just won the Super Bowl in '81.

The 49ers' players expected perfection, whether it was during a game or just blocking sleds (right), wind sprints, and simple handoff drills.

RONNIE LOTT: If you were a guy who just played on special teams, you felt that you had to play up to *your* standard, play up to *your* abilities. And by doing that, you would be just one piece of the puzzle that would allow us to win.

It was incubated after we lost an early season game to Atlanta in 1981, getting annihilated (34-17). Bill said that we couldn't play like that any longer, that we had to play to another standard, that we had to be able to beat our opponent to the punch.

BRENT JONES: It was a surreal experience my first summer, getting in the huddle (in 1987). I mean, I started off like the seventh- or eighth-string tight end and worked my way up. I had a couple of chances in summer camp to get in with the first unit. To sit and see Roger next to you, and Dwight, and Joe calling the plays—you felt like whipping out a pen and asking for their autographs.

I mean, I went crazy when Bill Walsh told me I'm doing a great job, and keep it up, I had a chance to make the team. That was like midway through camp, and that was the only thing that got me through the rest of training camp. Bill Walsh even knowing my name was phenomenal.

MIKE WALTER: You'd watch guys such as Roger Craig run the football, and they'd just be running a little nothing handoff drill. And the average back would run 20 yards and turn around, go back to the huddle. Every play, Roger Craig would just high-knee all the way down to the end of the field, to the

grass—70 yards every play. It was inspiring to see these guys who were already great, and how hard they worked. During 104-degree weather in training camp, to watch Jerry Rice run wind sprints after everyone else had gone in, you know? There weren't a lot of teams that would do that stuff.

JESSE SAPOLU: We made the playoffs every year, so we always were drafting in the bottom of the first round, and many times we didn't have a first-round pick. For us to be able to maintain that winning tradition and continue the magic was something we took pride in. We created a chemistry and a winning standard that we always referred to as the 49er standard.

RONNIE LOTT: When you play on great teams, or when you play on teams that want to be great, it's amazing how many people want to buy in to the cause. It's very difficult when you go to other teams that don't understand what the cause is all about. Sometimes the cause could be as simple as just getting along with another teammate. Or the cause could be as simple as making sure you're gonna constantly communicate. Whatever the cause is, you've gotta get people to buy in to it.

RANDY CROSS: We never wanted to have a winning season. We never wanted to win the division. We never wanted to win the conference. We wanted to win the world championship. And if we didn't do that, then we hadn't completely succeeded.

Hands were raised in triumph in the locker room at Super Bowl XXIII, moments after the 49ers had achieved their goal.

RONNIE LOTT: When we beat the Broncos in the last Super Bowl that I was with the 49ers (Super Bowl XXIV), I remember walking off the field not believing that we had played the perfect game. Even though the score represented what it did (a 55-10 drubbing by the 49ers), we felt that we still hadn't played up to our capabilities.

GUY MCINTYRE: It was like everyone was gunning for us, and we had to go out there and defend. We couldn't take anybody lightly. Because it was

you knock off the Niners and that just increased your market share right there. If you knock off the Niners, you're a contender.

RONNIE LOTT: When we were ahead with the 49ers, that's when people were nervous. That's when we panicked. Most teams, when they're ahead they relax. Vice-versa, when the Niners were down, our guys were relaxed. They knew the ebb and flow would change.

CHAPTER THIRTEEN

AN INCOMPARABLE RECEIVER

he 1985 draft was a classic case of the rich getting richer. The 49ers had just won their second Super Bowl, and were scheduled to draft last in the first round. But Bill Walsh had become enamored with a lanky wide receiver who had accumulated surreal numbers at tiny Mississippi Valley State. So Walsh traded his first two picks for New England's first-round choice, the sixteenth selection overall (the teams also swapped third-round picks as part of the deal).

The Patriots wound up with Trevor Matich and Ben Thomas. The 49ers got Jerry Rice. He struggled somewhat during his rookie year, dropping numerous passes, but largely because of his addition the San Francisco offense was about to explode.

Whether catching passes from Joe Montana or Steve Young (or anyone else, for that matter), Rice became a revelation in the NFL. Though undeniably athletic, his production far outstripped even his physical tools—his speed, size, and leaping ability. He excelled through endless repetition, running the most precise and hard-to-predict routes of any receiver in the league. By the time he wrapped up his seventeenth season, with the Raiders in 2001, Rice's career records for receptions (1,364), receiving yards (20,386), and touchdowns (196) looked unreachable—and he wasn't done.

Blessed with great natural tools and an outstanding work ethic, Jerry Rice set records that may never be equaled.

ROGER CRAIG: I saw what kind of potential Jerry Rice had in his rookie year. I was already training every offseason. I said, "Jerry, why don't you come work with me, man?"

He never lifted weights before. He didn't know how to lift or how to run or anything. I was a track guy. I used to teach him how to breathe, how to relax when we did our workouts. Basically we worked out together eight or nine years. It was like he got better and better throughout the offseason. Now he's almost legendary with it.

DWIGHT HICKS: You could tell that Jerry was gonna be a very special receiver. He worked very hard in practice. Let's face it, when he worked against our secondary, he worked against the best defensive backs in the league. We had a lot of great players. But just watching Jerry and his work ethic and what time he put into just being an outstanding receiver...you just knew something good was gonna happen with Jerry.

FREDDIE SOLOMON: Being in the system Bill Walsh developed was a plus for every wideout. Jerry's abilities spoke for themselves. We threw the ball, and he was a target who didn't mind going and making things happen. It didn't hurt having a quarterback like Montana throwing to him—to me, he was the best ever. And having Steve Young, another great quarterback, helped too.

DWIGHT HICKS: I remember a time when we were going to a chamber of commerce luncheon in the city. Jerry came and he sat with me on the bus. He had dropped some balls, and the 49ers were looking for better things from him. He sat down (feeling) a little down, and he said, "Dwight, can I talk to you?"

Rice saluted 49ers fans after a touchdown reception in 1987—1 of an NFL-record 22 he had that season.

I said, "Yeah. What's up, Jerry?"

He thought that (fellow wide receivers) Freddie Solomon and Dwight Clark were gonna sort of take him under their wing. Jerry was the future. And I guess they didn't do that as much as they should

Rice read the game program prior to Super Bowl XXIII, in which he would be named the game's MVP.

have, and he was a little down about that. And I just told him, "Jerry, you know what? You can't worry about that. I think that's stupid of them not to. But if you just keep working as hard as you're working right now, things will take care of themselves." I said, "You have a lot of talent. You're a very good receiver." And I said, "You just keep working hard and things will take care of themselves."

And geez, they did more than that. He's one of the most accomplished receivers in NFL history.

FREDDIE SOLOMON: I don't think he was down. It was a new system, and he was adjusting. Bill wanted to play him. And we tried to make sure he was prepared.

Watching him on the field, you could see he was big, he was quick, he had big hands, and he ran very good routes. I thought if he could be consistent (keep his body in top shape), and if he would work at his game, there was no telling what he could accomplish. He did that. He worked hard. He stayed focused on getting the job done.

ROGER CRAIG: Jerry Rice definitely added a dimension to our team. He added a breakaway threat. It opened our whole offense up, made our offense vertical. Defenses couldn't cover me and then cover Jerry, too. If they tried to drop the linebackers in the zone, then I'd eat 'em up.

The fans relished a familiar sight in 1989, when Rice scored against the Chicago Bears on a 29-yard pass from Joe Montana.

CHAPTER FOURTEEN

1988:
TRIBULATION
AND REDEMPTION

O f all the 49ers' championship seasons, 1988 involved the most turmoil.

After 11 weeks, the team's record stood at 6-5, perilously close to playoff elimination. What's more, Bill Walsh and Joe Montana seemed to be engaged in a quiet feud. Montana still simmered over his benching during a disheartening loss to Minnesota in the 1987 playoffs. Walsh sat Montana for a stretch in '88, too, first because of an elbow injury, later because of dysentery, and sometimes because of performance. Outside factions began to line up behind Montana or his replacement, Steve Young, who had been acquired by trade in 1987.

San Francisco regrouped to finish 10-6, edging the Rams and Saints for the NFC West title. After two impressive playoff victories, the season reverted to form and the 49ers found themselves locked in a fitful Super Bowl XXIII battle with Cincinnati.

The end of that game was the epitome of the Walsh-Montana era. Taking possession with 3:10 to play, the quarterback coolly guided his team 92 yards, climaxed by a perfect pass to John Taylor for a touchdown and a 20-16 victory. Three days after the game, a weary Walsh announced his retirement.

Joe Montana and Bill Walsh didn't always see eye to eye in their sometimes tumultuous journey through the 1988 season.

HARRIS BARTON: We were 6-5 going into a Sunday-night game versus Washington....I remember guys sitting around the training room at that point, making their plans for the offseason. It was a situation the 49ers weren't familiar with. And there was a group of veterans that called a team meeting. Obviously I was too young of a guy to be a big influence on that team, other than playing. Ronnie Lott and Randy Cross and others stood up and said, "[Expletive], let's do it. Let's do it for ourselves. We're in this thing. We've got a chance. And we're a much better team than we're showing. Let's go out there and get this thing done one game at a time."

In all my years in the NFL, it's really the only team meeting that I can ever remember that didn't turn into a bitch session or a gripe session or a he-said-this and he-said-that type of thing. It was actually productive. We set goals. Milestones were put down, and milestones were met. And the next thing you know, we went in and had a great end to the season.

BILL WALSH: The championship game against Chicago in 1988 was a great game for Joe in those weather conditions. His attitude toward it and the whole team's attitude toward it—that was big.

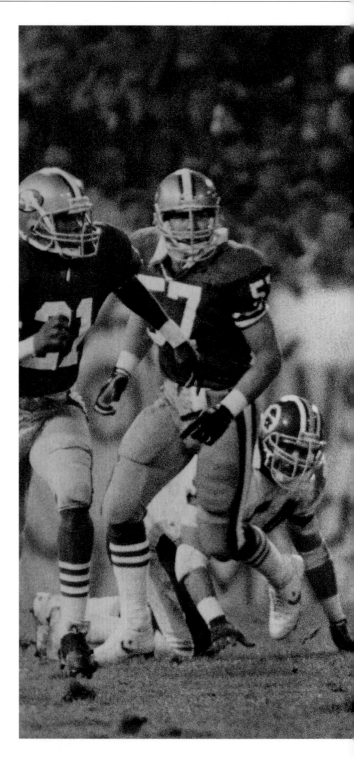

John Taylor, who returned a punt 95 yards for a touchdown against the Washington Redskins in week 12 (right), also made the game-winning touchdown reception in Super Bowl XXIII.

Joe Montana was alone with his thoughts in the moments before Super Bowl XXIII.

HARRIS BARTON: It was a Sunday game and we flew into Chicago on Friday. And it was warm. It was 50 degrees. And we thought, "Hey, this is great." Then we heard there was a storm front moving in. And the Chicago papers were all over it: "We're used to this. We're gonna go out there and kill these guys."...

I remember their offensive line had the reputation of baring their arms to show how tough they were. Our offensive linemen all put sleeves on

because it was bitter cold. When you walked out of the locker room that first time and took that first breath, the steam in front of your face made sure you couldn't see what was going on. They had the field covered. They pulled the cover off, and it didn't feel so bad. We went through warm-ups all right. But when we got on the field, we recognized that all their guys were wearing tennis shoes. We didn't really understand why until, maybe in the first quarter, Joe dropped back to throw a pass, seven-step drop, and he hit the big C that was painted in the middle of the field. As he came across it and tried to plant, he actually slipped because all the moisture in the painted C had turned to ice. It was a big ice C out there. So we all sprinted in and changed into tennis shoes.

BILL WALSH: I had made up my mind some weeks before that I would retire at the end of the season. But I didn't think that I should bring that to the team. The team had enough to think about. They were concentrating on their opponents. We were on a down-the-wire stretch to make the play-offs and to qualify for the Super Bowl. And for me to add that to it would be dealing in the dramatic....Prior to (Super Bowl XXIII), I didn't want the players to think they had to win one for Bill, or win one for the coach because it was my last game.

I can recall taking a walk around the stadium prior to the game. To be honest, I broke down a little bit, all by myself, nobody knowing why, because I knew this would be my last game.

RANDY CROSS: I'm asked constantly which is my favorite team, which is my favorite Super Bowl. And for me it's impossible to differentiate. Because there was so much special about doing it the first time in Super Bowl XVI. And the best team I ever played on was the one that won Super Bowl XIX. And there is no better way, if you're in any sport or any endeavor—you know, the old let's-go-out-on-top. I mean, in my last game we won the

Super Bowl on our last drive. Duh. Does it get any better than that?

JESSE SAPOLU: To be able to go 92 yards to win the world championship, knowing how focused I was and how focused the 10 other guys were on making sure that each one-eleventh of (the offense) were doing our job....And to be able to go down there and get it done was very, very satisfying.

BILL WALSH: We didn't call any (plays) that we hadn't executed (earlier in the game) until the last play. So they were plays we knew we could count on....But there wasn't time to do anything except do my job and have each player do his job, and hope the chemistry was there. And it certainly was. Joe Montana was brilliant, as was everyone else on the field.

JOE MONTANA: Against Cincinnati, the touchdown pass to John Taylor—I did that 18 million times in my backyard as a kid growing up.

RANDY CROSS: (NBC announcer) Bob Costas made a comment to me (in the postgame locker room) about how I could have been the goat because I had a bad snap on a field-goal attempt, and I had an illegal receiver downfield (penalty) on the last drive. Did that even enter my mind? And I could have pounded his little butt for saying it. It was like, "Gee, no kidding. Thanks for bringing it up."

CHAPTER FIFTEEN

THORNS AMONG THE ROSES

t seems odd to speak of disappointments for a team that captured an unprecedented five Super Bowl trophies in 14 years. Then again, that means that the 49ers came up short nine seasons during that time frame. Many of them were narrow failures, including four losses in NFC Championship Games (and not including four subsequent postseason losses between 1995 and 1998).

These near misses nagged at the team, at the owner who demanded perfection, at Bill Walsh and his exacting staff of coaches, and at the fans who had come to expect easy victories. Most of all, they nagged at the players who knew how close they had come to an even more impressive legacy.

The 49ers were stunned in the 1986 playoffs when they trailed the Giants 28-3 at halftime en route to a 49-3 defeat.

KEITH FAHNHORST: You hate to say it, but we were starting to get a little spoiled with success. Once you win the Super Bowl, anything less than that really leaves a bitter taste in your mouth.

JESSE SAPOLU: I can remember losing in the NFC Championship Game, and it was almost like we never won a regular-season game through the whole season. That's how hard we took it.

EDDIE DEBARTOLO: (Former wide receiver) Freddie Solomon stopped by to say hello one day, and we were talking a little bit about some of our successes. We went through some of the playoffs and championship games. My God, we had a shot at winning more than five titles. We might have been able to win seven or eight Super Bowls, except for a little fumble here and a little mistake there.

JESSE SAPOLU: When people ask me how many Super Bowl rings I have, I don't mean to show a disappointed face, but I just say, "Four," very casually.

And they say, "You don't look very excited about it."

And I tell people, "Well, I lost five [including 1997] NFC Championship Games."

That's a lot of big games to lose....When I look back on my career, I should be sitting here with at least six, maybe seven Super Bowl rings, if some of the things had fallen our way.

HARRIS BARTON: We should've won more. Why did we not win more? We should have three-peated. It sounds like sour grapes. But that's what was instilled by the ownership and Mr. DeBartolo: We're gonna win this thing every year.

KEITH FAHNHORST: When the New York Giants beat us (49-3 in a 1986 divisional playoff game), that was disappointing. Joe missed some games because of a back injury that year. He came back and really played well and got us in the playoffs. We had a huge game against the Rams the last game of the year to win the division. We had really overcome a lot. So it was disappointing we got beat the way we did in New York.

BILL WALSH: The biggest disappointment had to be the 1987 loss to Minnesota in the (divisional) playoffs. We were 13-2 that year. We clearly had the best team. We had great momentum. And they caught us at the wrong time (Minnesota won 36-24).

They had some luck, and some great performances by players, and we stuttered and stumbled and couldn't believe what was happening. We got behind and couldn't catch up. We made a run at it in the second half, but we were too far behind. That game haunts me still today. It caused sort of a break between the owner and me for a short period of time. It was just an absolute tragedy.

Ronnie Lott sat motionless in front of his locker after a 24-21 loss to Washington in the 1983 NFC Championship Game.

MIKE WALTER: We all but had our bags packed and were going to (another Super Bowl as we played the final moments) against the New York Giants in the NFC Championship Game (in 1990), when Roger Craig fumbled the ball. We were running the clock out, and I'm thinking, "We're going again." And right before our eyes, it just slipped away and disappeared. That was a tough one.

BRENT JONES: In '91 we were probably the best team in the NFL, and we did not go to the playoffs. We were 10-6 and we didn't make it. We had some midseason injuries (including those to Jones, Steve Young, and defensive end Pierce Holt), and we kind of slumped before finishing strong. We beat the Bears 52-14 on the last Monday night of the season ....The Redskins won the Super Bowl (XXVI) with an average team. And we would have just ripped them.

KEENA TURNER: After we won Super Bowl XVI, the next year (1982) was a strike-shortened year. We went 3-6 and didn't make the playoffs. The Rams beat us the last game of the year. And that offseason was one of my most embarrassing....

But it put (my football) career in this perspective: The years are very separate. One year has absolutely nothing to do with another. And how you per-

The players wore the look of dejection in 1985 when their season ended with a 17-3 loss to the Giants in a wild-card game.

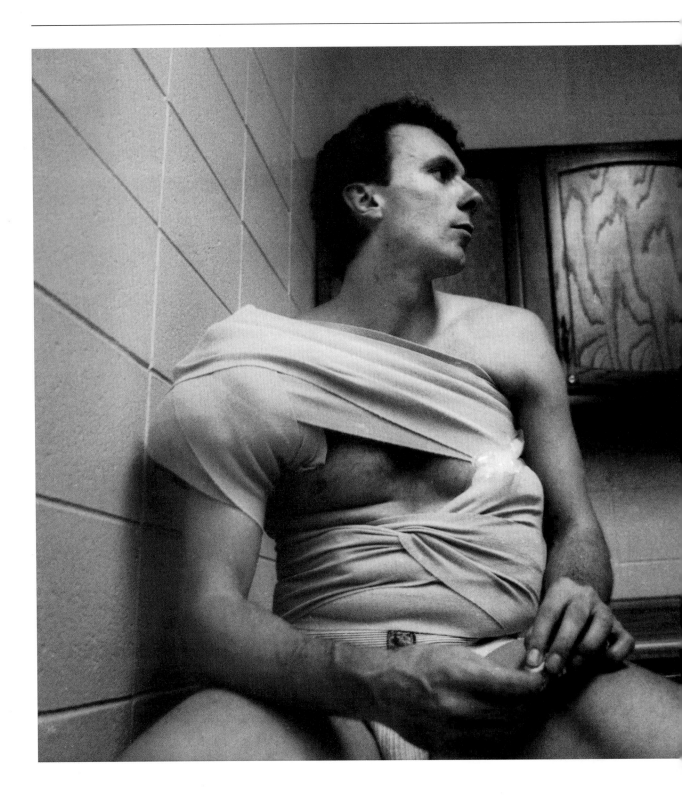

form in a given year has nothing to do with how you'll perform the next year. I think that was a lesson for the team. That year (1982) had as much to do with building what was here as when we won.

RONNIE LOTT: It's not whether we lost in the playoffs, or we lost going for three (consecutive) Super Bowls. The greatest disappointment is when we didn't play up to our standard. Those things happened every year. I've never watched tapes of the game that we lost to the Giants. I've never watched that game we lost to the Vikings. You try and block those moments out of your memory because you're almost embarrassed to even think about them.

The pain of defeat was more than emotional for Joe Montana, who ended the 1985 season with ice packs on his shoulder and his rib cage.

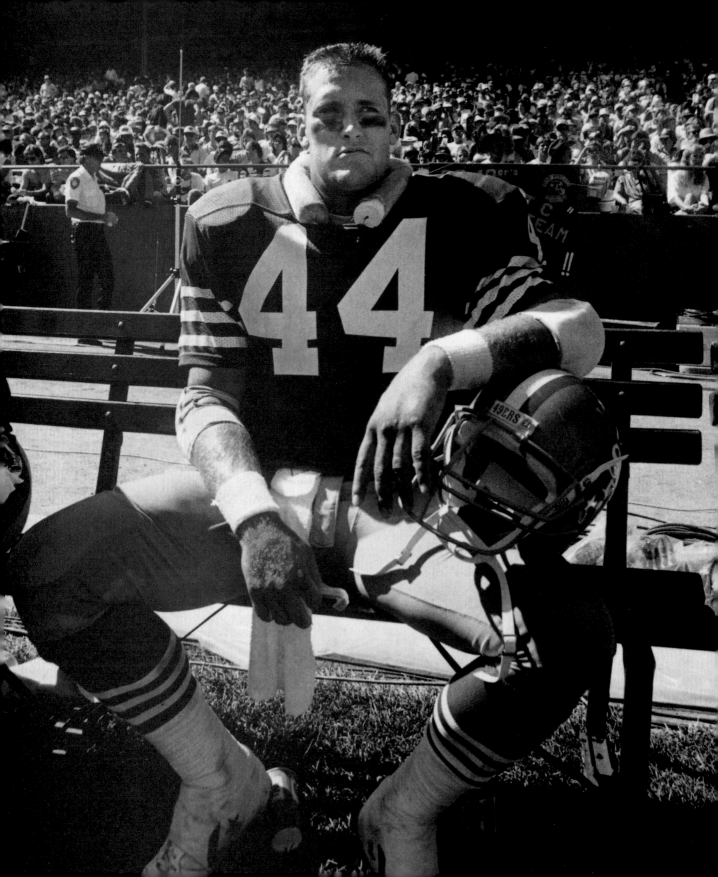

CHAPTER SIXTEEN

THE UNSUNG HEROES

'WITHOUT THEM'

I n the retrospective book *NFL's Greatest,* published in 2000, Joe Montana, Ronnie Lott, Jerry Rice, and Steve Young all were counted among the 100 greatest players in league history. You can't have a 14-year run of dominance without that kind of star power.

In basketball or baseball, a few all-stars might be enough to carry a team to greatness.

In the NFL, they won't come close without contributions from the entire 45-man roster. For every Montana there is Tom Rathman, nailing blitzers and catching short passes in a pinch. For every Lott there is Dan Bunz, coming up with tackles that help to turn a Super Bowl. The role players are recalled fondly, and gratefully, in San Francisco.

Fullback Tom Rathman was the sort of overlooked role player who did his job without any fanfare.

ROGER CRAIG: There were a lot of guys on our team who were unsung heroes. There were a lot of guys who never got the credit for some of the things they did, who were a big part of our system. A lot of us got the headlines—me, Montana, Rice, Ronnie, we were the big four.

But there were guys like Billy Ring. He sold out on special teams. And if there was a certain player he had to go in and block, like for a first down, they would call his number. There were guys like Ron Ferrari, who would sell out on the kickoff team and throw his body to the wolves. You had guys like Rick Gervais, who was another solid player who meant a lot to our team. You had a guy like Milt McColl who played hard on special teams. There were a ton of guys who played huge roles in making it happen for us. A lot of guys who worked their butts off. Like Riki Ellison. Some people doubted whether he'd be able to make it in the NFL. He had four knee surgeries (in college), and he was out there crushing people at linebacker. Willie Harper was another one.

RANDY CROSS: When people look back and say, "What was one of the foundations? What was one of the true pillars of what Bill did in San Francisco?" They're going to look at Bobb McKittrick, our offensive line coach, and say, "That wouldn't have happened without somebody like that."...

Assistant coach Bobb McKittrick was described by his offensive linemen as the best teacher in the business.

John McVay (left) had the front-office expertise to mediate any differences between Eddie DeBartolo (center) and Bill Walsh.

To me, he is the best argument you can make, over this time and the last 10 years or so, as to why assistant coaches should be in the Hall of Fame. There are plenty of guys with over 100 wins who don't match up against a lot of assistants, from McKittrick to (famed defensive coordinator Fritz) Shurmur.

GUY MCINTYRE: It's easy to find the number ones and number twos, and sometimes the number threes. But to find the later-round draft choices, and for them to come in and work out, to bring them along, and to be efficient in what you're trying to do, is a credit to the guy in charge of them. I would like to give a lot of credit to Bobb. I don't know how many offensive line coaches have coached five Super Bowl offensive lines.

BILL MCPHERSON: This guy did magic tricks at times. I mean, he had some good players, but not a lot of high draft picks. Harris Barton was the only number-one pick he had....Bobb was one of the all-time great ones in terms of his work habits and his knowledge of the game, and how he'd get people ready to play in the game, technique-wise. I think he was the best teacher of technique I've ever been around. He didn't want to be a head coach. He wanted to be with his guys.

JOHN MCVAY: I remember one year during the strike, Bobb had intestinal cancer. They wanted to operate on him. He said, "I can't get operated on.

What if they end the strike tomorrow? I'll be out."

I said, "Bobb, the hell with the strike. Get the surgery."

"Nah," he said, "I can't do that."

And he didn't. He waited until the season was over. He's a hero. Right down in the coaches' locker room today, there's a locker with his picture in it. His clothes are hanging in it.

BRENT JONES: John Taylor, because of his refusal to speak to the media, I think never got the accolades. And he was a phenomenal athlete, a phenomenal player....Go back and look at his numbers when he was healthy and involved, and he made some things happen.

HARRIS BARTON: JT was it. Here's a guy who was a great punt returner. I mean, just a *great* punt returner. And the coaching staff couldn't put him back there because they were scared to get him hurt. Here's a guy, we'd run a sweep and he'd just knock the crap out of a linebacker. He was good in the locker room....I can't ever remember him having a big drop or a big fumble. Just a tremendous football player.

BRENT JONES: If you wanna talk about an unsung hero, John McVay is a guy who gets pushed to the back a lot. I think most people in football felt like for the first 10, 12, 15 years, he was the best there was. He wasn't a vocal guy. And I think he was probably as instrumental as anybody.

CARMEN POLICY: I worked with (McVay) since he came. He's a perfect example of stability and cohesiveness. He had no separate agenda to that of the 49ers. And he had a tranquilizing effect during times of stress.

BILL McPHERSON: Eddie and Bill would have some exchanges. I think McVay was the mediator. Here's a guy who had been an NFL head coach, and been a (college) player. He knew how to rock and roll with this thing.

KEENA TURNER: John Ayers was a guy who embodied what it's all about. I miss him. So many times we talk about the guys who everybody remembers. And there's just so many guys like John who we forget. And we shouldn't. You don't win without them. You don't have Super Bowls. I mean, you can't do it without a Joe Montana or a Ronnie Lott. But you can't do it without John Ayers, Keith Fahnhorst, Lawrence Pillers, Dwaine Board.

BILL McPHERSON: Dwaine Board played here 10 years. I mean, this guy played defensive end at 248 pounds. I remember when we first went to the 3-4 defense, John Madden was doing our game at Candlestick. He said, "Hear you guys are running the three-four. Who are your ends?"

I said, "Right end is gonna be Dwaine Board."

"Oh, no, you can't play that defense with him."

Remember, when Madden coached, he had those big defensive ends. "Who's your other end?"

I said, "[Jim] Stuckey [at 251 pounds]."

"Oh, my God, you're gonna get killed!"

Hell, Dwaine Board played right end for 10 years. He was one of the smartest players I ever had, and very productive. I scouted him when he was a linebacker at North Carolina A&T, when I was coaching in Philly.

I used to turn my back on Dwaine Board. I wouldn't take him out of the game. He'd be out there looking at me, tapping his helmet like he wanted to get out. I'd just turn my back. But you knew he was gonna be there every day.

JOHN McVAY: Jesse Sapolu was a quiet leader and a strong personality. He never tried to dominate, but always tried to offer strength and support.

ERIC WRIGHT: Why ain't Fred Dean in the Hall of Fame? I don't know. He wreaked havoc on offensive linemen. Late in a game—Joe Montana, Fred Dean, Ronnie Lott. If all three of those guys made plays, we were guaranteed to win games.

Dwaine Board, at 248 pounds, was undersized for his position, but that didn't stop him from flourishing for 10 NFL seasons.

CHAPTER SEVENTEEN

WEATHERING THE TRANSITION

THE STRUCTURE AND THE SYSTEM DID NOT CHANGE.

Bill Walsh began his coaching career in San Francisco with a 2-14 season. He went out on top, stepping down as head coach after leading the team to victory in Super Bowl XXIII. More changes would follow during the next few years, including the departures of Ronnie Lott and Roger Craig as Plan B free agents in 1991, the trade of Charles Haley to Dallas in 1992, and, most devastating to 49ers' fans, the trade of Joe Montana to Kansas City in 1993.

Other franchises might have plummeted into those dreaded "rebuilding years" in the face of such rapid turnover. Defying the odds, the 49ers remained upright. George Seifert would win two Super Bowls as Walsh's successor, and all of the other key losses would be ably replaced.

The consistency that the 49ers showed through the transition years is testament to the depth of talent they had waiting in the wings, and to the proven organizational structure that existed at the time—and that still remains today.

A remarkable era ended after Super Bowl XXIII, when Bill Walsh stepped down as 49ers head coach.

JESSE SAPOLU: I tell people there were only two teams that won five Super Bowls, the 49ers and the Dallas Cowboys. The difference is that the Dallas Cowboys' five came from two completely different generations. And the 49ers, it's almost like a continuation from the run of the eighties into the nineties.

JOHN MCVAY: George was Bill's hand-picked successor. That's who Bill wanted to have the job. At that time, there were some other names—Jimmy Johnson—bounced around. And Bill was extremely instrumental in convincing the DeBartolos that George was their guy.

BILL WALSH: George had more tenure than anybody. He was the senior assistant. He had been with me virtually the entire time, and had served as defensive coordinator during that time while I managed the offense. So he had more individual responsibility and authority than anyone else....Now George was receiving, as were other coaches on our staff, job opportunities elsewhere. We were sort of a hot item at that time. So I had to push pretty hard and pretty quickly to get George on board as head coach. There were some other candidates outside the organization.

George Seifert was a logical successor to Bill Walsh, and he demonstrated as much with a victory in Indianapolis in his first game as the 49ers' head coach.

JOHN MCVAY: In the pecking order it was, here's Bill, and here's George (hand held slightly below), and here's the rest of the assistants (substantially lower). It wasn't like we were going to Southside High School to hire the guy. This is a guy who had been here for nine years, had been part of the success of those first three Super Bowls, who had coached the secondary on that '81 team with three rookies and a free agent. It was a very natural progression.

MICHAEL ZAGARIS: The first year (after Walsh), the players wanted to win it for him (Seifert), to prove it wasn't just Coach Walsh or Mr. D. It was the team. And they kicked ass.

BILL MCPHERSON: The structure and the system did not change. I worked with George when he was the defensive backs coach and when he was the coordinator. When he became the head coach, I became the defensive coordinator. But nothing in the structure really changed.

BRENT JONES: The 49er way has always been to make transition as seamless as possible. So George didn't do anything different. The schedule was the same the whole time I was there....George came in and nothing really felt that different, you know,

The 49ers' most publicized transition was at quarterback, where Steve Young (right) received the unenviable assignment of replacing the legendary Joe Montana.

Montana was just one of several stars to depart.

other than a different head guy getting up in front and talking to you....George didn't bring in new coaches. We still had the same offensive coordinator. And part of the success, when he did bring in a new coordinator—when Mike Holmgren left and Mike Shanahan came in—he didn't say, "Okay, Mike, we're gonna run your style of offense."

Mike had to come in and learn the West Coast Offense....We had coaches and players adapt to the way we did things, rather than vice-versa. I think that's probably been the biggest ingredient for success in the transition.

JESSE SAPOLU: When Randy Cross retired, (center) Fred Quillan retired, and Ronnie Lott went to the Raiders, players like Guy McIntyre, (tackle) Steve Wallace, and me were already veteran enough to know what kind of standard was expected of the San Francisco 49ers. And we were able to keep that going until players were able to come and go through free agency. It's hard to put that standard in a bottle, so to speak, because the game is different now.

CARMEN POLICY: The transition from Bill to George Seifert coincided with the transition of the business. The league was becoming more businesslike. There was a different approach to marketing and stadium economics, a new way of doing business. Eddie refused to be part of a team with its best days behind it. Free agency and the cap came along. This was one of our biggest challenges. We had the highest payroll in the league at that time, and the cap system was designed to hit the high-payroll teams.

EDDIE DEBARTOLO: Joe Montana and Ronnie Lott are two of my best friends. And they both left. Joe went to Kansas City, Ronnie went to Oakland.

RONNIE LOTT: I think that Bill (Walsh) realized that when you want to keep a dynasty going, you have to make tough decisions, that you have to do what's unpopular. There's a lot of validity to why he did that, and why it worked....Everybody thinks it was George, and they say it was Carmen. But the catalyst was Bill because Bill knew you had to replace your older players. And you had to do it not when the player was ready, but when the player was on his downside. And there's nothing wrong with that. For me, a lot of people said, "Weren't you mad at Bill?" And I thought, "I can't be mad at him. I got my career to take care of."

You look forward.

CHAPTER EIGHTEEN

1989:
A TEAM
ON A MISSION

fter the roller-coaster ride of 1988, the '89 season was more like a bullet train. Wide receiver John Taylor and tight end Brent Jones joined the starting lineup as complements to Jerry Rice, and Joe Montana was at the pinnacle of his abilities. The defense, meanwhile, held a majority of opponents to fewer than 20 points in George Seifert's first year as head coach.

The 49ers lost two home games, to the Rams and Packers, by a total of five points. Their road record was spotless. The Rams, behind a big season by quarterback Jim Everett, emerged as San Francisco's greatest threat. But the 49ers put an end to the uprising by hounding Everett in a convincing NFC Championship Game victory. That was part of a postseason run that saw the 49ers outscore their three opponents by 100 points (126-26).

The 49ers saved their most awesome display for last. Montana and Rice hooked up for a touchdown less than five minutes into Super Bowl XXIV, and Seifert's team galloped to a 55-10 rout of Denver—the most lopsided victory in Super Bowl history.

Linebacker Matt Millen (54) introduced himself to the Giants' Maurice Carthon in a Monday night victory.

HARRIS BARTON: That was a team on a mission. The mission was: Let's show everybody we can win this thing, go back to back. George Seifert was the new coach, and the veterans on the team wanted to make sure they carried on the tradition Bill Walsh had put in. And that team was locked and loaded from day one.

GUY MCINTYRE: We came in with the same focus and purpose as always—get in the playoffs.

Don't be afraid to say you're shooting for the Super Bowl:…"That's right, this is what we're doing. And we're gonna go out and work toward doing that each day." To get there and play a game against Denver like we did, it was just great.

RONNIE LOTT: We really focused on writing a new book, from the standpoint that you didn't hear a lot of people talk about Bill Walsh that year. You didn't hear a lot of people discuss the year before.

New coach George Seifert received a game ball from Eddie DeBartolo after registering his first victory, a 30-24 decision over Indianapolis.

George Seifert talked and Joe Montana listened during a time out in Philadelphia, where the 49ers rallied for a 38-28 victory.

The focus was more on the moment. To me, that allowed us to think not about repeating, but just trying to win. It's almost as if we didn't do anything the year before.

It was incredible for a team to do that. It says a lot about George Seifert. It says a lot about the great players. But it also says a lot about everyone in that organization, from the secretaries to the equipment people. Everybody felt that last year was over with, and we have to write a new book.

MATT MILLEN: Montana was on another planet, another level. I distinctly remember prior to (Super Bowl XXIV), that the ball didn't hit the ground one time in practice. It was phenomenal. And I asked him prior to the game, "How many points could you get?"

He said, "A hundred if they let me."

He didn't say it with an air of cockiness. He said it matter-of-fact, with a little smile on his face. He knew. He was confident.

Years later, when I was doing television, I had a

chance to do a Denver Broncos game, and I was sitting down with John Elway. We were talking about it, and I told him that story, and he shook his head and said to me, "When our scout team ran against our defense, [the defense] couldn't stop 'em." He said he and (backup quarterback Gary) Kubiak just looked at each other and said, "Oh, no."

JOE MONTANA: What sticks in my mind the most is years later when I was in Kansas City (in 1993), and we were getting ready to play Denver. (Backup quarterback) Dave Krieg and I and (third stringer) Matt Blundin and (offensive coordinator) Paul Hackett were in the room watching the tape of Super Bowl XXIV. And I forgot how bad I played in the beginning. And Dave Krieg said to me, "You were the MVP of this game?"

I said, "Yeah, it gets a little bit better as we go along."

KEENA TURNER: The weird thing was, at the end of my career, winning Super Bowl XXIV, in a lot of ways was anticlimactic. You keep pushing throughout your career for more. There's always more. And maybe I knew it was close to the end, but there's always the expectation of more. And to win a Super Bowl the way we did, and to feel that it was a little anticlimactic, is something that always has kind of stood out for me.

The 49ers took pride in rallying around their new coach, winning their first Super Bowl without Bill Walsh at the controls.

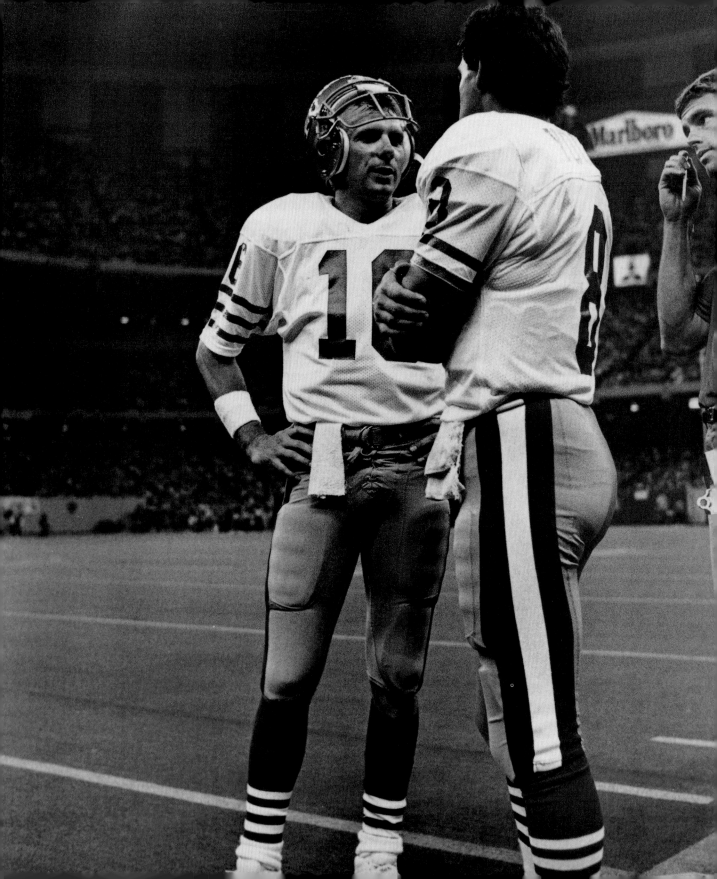

CHAPTER NINETEEN

REPLACING A LEGEND

he 49ers had a superb but sometimes brittle quarterback in Joe Montana, so Bill Walsh jumped at the chance to acquire Steve Young from Tampa Bay (for second and fourth-round draft choices, plus cash) in 1987.

Young couldn't have presented a more striking contrast to Montana. He was strong, an imposing athletic presence who threw the ball left-handed. And while Montana came to the NFL as a marginal prospect who shot his way up the ladder, Young left Brigham Young with seemingly limitless potential, then watched his career waste away in the USFL and with the lowly Buccaneers. When he got to San Francisco, Young was so used to running for his life that he had trouble adapting to the precision required of a quarterback in the West Coast offense.

Meanwhile, Young suffered from what was perceived as a personal rivalry with Montana. Though most 49ers insiders insist there was no true ill will, the fans and media of San Francisco vocally took sides—and most of them sided with Montana. Even as Young led the NFL in passing every year from 1991-93, he had local detractors who classified him as a statistical wonder who couldn't win big games. That would change in 1994, when he not only set an NFL record for passer rating but also led the team to Super Bowl XXIX.

By the time a series of concussions knocked Young out of the league in 1999, the 49ers fans knew they were saying goodby to one of the all-time greats. His career passer rating of 96.8 was the best in NFL history entering the 2002 season.

Even though they were undeniable rivals, Joe Montana and Steve Young were teammates first.

ROGER CRAIG: When Steve Young first came in, he'd look at the primary (receiver) and he would freak out. If the primary was covered, he'd take off running.

BRENT JONES: But the great thing he had when he was backing up Joe was time—time to watch Joe, time to watch the offense develop, time to get an idea of how to play quarterback. He was really a running back who could throw the ball. And he became so disciplined. I've never seen such a transition—and I've seen a lot of quarterbacks throughout the years on other teams— where a guy basically reinvented himself. He wanted his running to be an asset, but he did not want to be a running quarterback. He wanted to be a pocket passer, read the progression, know the offense, and know the defenses. And he studied harder than anybody I've ever seen.

Young relaxed at his locker in 1994—the season in which he climbed out from Montana's shadow by leading the 49ers to a Super Bowl title.

GUY McINTYRE: It's a tough act to follow. Here you have Joe, who's spanned over a decade with the 49ers and brought them from famine to feast....And it's hard to walk into that and try to fill those shoes. If you don't win right away or you don't win by a big margin, then it's hard. It's like the guy trying to fill Vince Lombardi's spot. What do you do? I mean, how many championships can you win? And you can't win 'em fast enough.

Steve probably was the prototypical quarterback. You know— big guy, strong looking. Joe wasn't—skinny legs, third-round draft choice....And here you have Steve, the million-dollar baby from day one— the USFL and all of that, cream of the crop. Then he's coming in, trying to replace a legend. I'm sure it was hard. I think almost anybody would struggle with that.

The quarterback rivalry heated up in a 1987 playoff game, when Young replaced a struggling Montana during a loss to Minnesota.

BRENT JONES: He's probably my best friend. I think he put an unbelievable amount of pressure on himself to live up to what Joe had done. And he probably wouldn't even make that admission today. But he did.

JOE MONTANA: The only problem I ever had was the push for Steve when I'd been having good years. I never understood that part of it. But I know exactly why Bill Walsh brought Steve in when I hurt my back (in 1986). He used it to motivate me— which is fine, too, when I look back on it.

HARRIS BARTON: It was blown up (in the media). Joe and Steve were competitors, and bitter competitors. But there's one thing I can tell you about both of them: It was never apparent on the outside. It was something the team never really recognized. And that's why the team was able to be so successful. Usually when you have competition like that, it will tear a team apart.

GUY MCINTYRE: Regardless of whether Joe's there or Steve's there, Guy has to do what Guy has to do for the 49ers to win. And everybody else who was up there on that line, same way. There was no

Steve Young, still something of an unknown commodity in the 1987 preseason, warmed up in the bowels of Los Angeles Memorial Coliseum before a game against the Los Angeles Raiders.

favorite. Hey, this is the person who's in there, we go with him. This is the 49ers. This is not Joe Montana's team or Steve Young's. This is the 49ers' team.

BRENT JONES: There are gonna be Joe people all the way, and there are some people who are Steve people. What can I say? If you're a fan of the 49ers, why can't you just appreciate that you got to spend all these years with two Hall of Fame quarterbacks?

DWIGHT CLARK: I think any time you follow a great Hall of Fame player like Joe Montana, you're gonna have your detractors. But Steve answered 'em. He took the team to the Super Bowl and dominated at the Super Bowl. Set records the whole year. It was just an amazing feat.

BRENT JONES: I think his natural demeanor, his confidence, and his abilities were apparent. So I think he always felt comfortable in the job. But he wasn't gonna give himself credit until he won that first Super Bowl.

Away from the spotlight of competition, Montana and Young found time for a casual conversation prior to a 1989 preseason game.

CHAPTER TWENTY

THE ROAR OF THE CROWD

ven in the days of Y.A. Tittle and Kezar Stadium, the 49ers were known to attract a loud and quirky crowd. The "Forty-Niner Faithful," they called themselves.

These fans had grown a bit surly by the time Bill Walsh showed up in 1979. When the 49ers began to win championships, however, the faithful jumped on board and never fell off. They turned tailgating into a sourdough-and-shrimp art form at Candlestick, and they lavished affection on the players. At the same time, they got used to winning and could be unforgiving when it didn't happen often enough, or impressively enough, to suit them.

Still, the people associated with the Eddie DeBartolo years look upon their relationship with the fans as one of the most satisfying aspects of the dynasty. And this human bond was cemented further by their fondness for the city of San Francisco, the greater Bay Area, and the many advantages they offer.

Confetti rained and cheers filled the air when the 49ers returned to San Francisco after Super Bowl XVI.

CARMEN POLICY: It's ironic. If you could parachute into the Bay Area and evaluate it with no former knowledge or exposure to that environment, you would think it might not be a fertile area for rabid, committed fans. There is a laid-back social view, and maybe not a great deal of respect for hostility. The intellectual level of the Bay Area is esoteric. But once you're there, when you understand the history, you can understand how the Bay Area could become mesmerized by the team once it started winning.

MICHAEL ZAGARIS: In 1981, as we really started to win, and the juggernaut started happening, fans started showing up at the airport after the game. After we beat Pittsburgh, we walked off the plane, there were thousands of people. That had never happened before. It was fresh and new. It was like your first love. People were just unbelievable. There was a passion I had never witnessed, and I started going to 49ers games when I was 8 years old.

BILL WALSH: The one singular moment was the first parade (after Super Bowl XVI). I was against the parade. I did not think anyone would bother to turn out during the day for a football team driving down the street. I just didn't think that was possible. So I really wasn't for it. I was very reluctant about it. And when we got off the plane after winning the

The 49ers were stunned at the size of the turnout for their first Super Bowl victory parade.

Super Bowl, they drove us around in these trolleys, and we turned the corner and started down the Embarcadero. There were just a handful of people on a corner, and a handful on the next corner. And I thought, "God, is this going to be embarrassing, going down Market Street, stalling traffic. No one's gonna be there!"

Well, we turned a corner and it was unbelievable. I don't know if there have ever been more people at one singular so-called parade or celebration, anywhere at any time. It was huge. Hanging from windows, on light posts, just thousands upon thousands of people, a hundred deep....It was mind-boggling. The noise and the excitement was unbelievable. We just had taken a quiet flight from Detroit and didn't expect anything like that. I was just stunned and awed by it.

The great thing about it for San Francisco is that the city was in some turmoil. There had been the two assassinations (of Mayor George Moscone and Supervisor Harvey Milk in November 1978). We had a real diverse community, each with its own political platform. And who could ever bring the city together? As great a city as it was, it was in conflict. And when we turned that corner and I looked in those people's eyes, I saw young people, tall people, short people, people of color, Asian people, much older people. I saw every cross section of people, all standing in unison, from the executives who came out of the office buildings, to the people who clean the streets, right next to each other, screaming. It was just the most electrifying moment I've ever had.

I think the 49ers brought the city together....And there were no detractors. There just weren't any. So whether it be in a gay section, whether it be in a predominately African-American section, whether it be in the affluent sections, there was one thing in common. That was the San Francisco 49ers.

EDDIE DEBARTOLO: Our family, both sides, came from Italian descent. Our grandparents, both my wife's and mine, were born in Italy. There's a large Italian population in San Francisco, and I was befriended so quickly and so easily. But not just Italians. I felt very much a part of the city....I always said we were in the entertainment business, and these people paid hard-earned money to come and see a show. And that's what it was.

CARMEN POLICY: I'm not sure a hard-hitting, grinding type of team that is often thought of as the stereotype of NFL football would really cause people of that area to become as committed to the 49ers. You have to do things with pizzazz. The West Coast offense has flair and finesse. There's a certain connection to execution. This team transcended typical brute strength, and I think people reveled in that. It's like watching the diminutive karate champion beat the heavyweight.

HARRIS BARTON: There's probably not a day or a week that goes by that somebody doesn't come up and shake my hand and say, "I know you've been out of the game for a while, but you guys were great.

Thanks for all those years." And you know what? That makes me feel good.

BILL WALSH: I don't know how it is with Don Shula and Chuck Noll, people like that who had some success. But in this community, I swear, everywhere I go, people of all ages thank me. It is unbelievable. Every place I go. They can be 21, they can be 71. They thank me, they thank me, they thank me. You hate to think you're getting used to it and sort of like it, but the gratification is unbelievable.

GUY MCINTYRE: I used to write God bless you (when signing autographs). And one day I saw a sign that said "God bless you, Guy" in the stands.

ROGER CRAIG: I had a letter from a fan from outside of Sacramento, California. The father had just gotten killed in a trucking accident. And the mother had sent me pictures of her two sons. The sons' names were Roger and Craig. They had named their sons after me. That was the most touching part of my career—that someone would love me that much, respect me that much, to name their two sons

after me. That was incredible. I ended up keeping in touch with them, sending them pictures, and visiting with them.

There was a mad scramble in the stands when Jerry Rice tossed a souvenir towel to fans.

BRENT JONES: It was an absolute love fest. People in the Bay Area live and breathe 49ers football.... People talked about it at work, it was on the radio station, it was in the shopping center. I mean, it was 49ers all the time. And it was great. I think we have a very, very refined fan base. Our fans can be as loud and as great and as fantastic as any fans can be. But they have high expectations.

BILL WALSH: The fans were so used to winning, and so used to a dominant football team, that they just expected it. And when it wasn't a dominant victory, we'd get some booing if we were ahead 7-0 at halftime. So it was pretty intense as to what they expected. And (San Francisco had) come from very little, football-wise. There'd been a couple of successful years with John Brodie (in the early 1970s), but historically they hadn't been able to get over the top. Once they were, I think they felt they deserved it. And they did.

JOE MONTANA: We used to get criticized if we'd win by less than a touchdown. We'd just say, "Okay, you can say what you want, but we still got a W." As they say, it's better to win ugly than to lose looking good.

DWIGHT CLARK: There's no place in the world like San Francisco. It's beautiful, it's cosmopolitan. It's got everything you could ever want. The diversity is incredible and the weather's perfect.

RANDY CROSS: The great thing about the Bay Area is that you don't have to love one thing about it. There's the city itself, there's the wine country, there's the Monterey Peninsula. It's got the best weather in the world. It's unbelievable. There's a reason it's the most expensive place to live on the planet.

HARRIS BARTON: People I played with came into the Bay Area right at the height of the 49ers power. We were representing the best city in the world. We were playing for the best owner in the world—arguably the best franchise ever in professional sports. And perhaps the most exciting economic conditions in the country. So the best weather, the best scenery, the best football team, the best business relationships, the best real-estate prices. The best of the best. It's still like that. That's why nobody leaves.

Despite a reputation for laid-back, intellectual fans, San Francisco bared its emotions in support of its football team.

CHAPTER TWENTY-ONE

PARADE OF RIVALS

he Cowboys have the Redskins. The Raiders have the Chiefs. The 49ers don't have one great rival, but there was plenty of enmity to go around during the dynasty.

For most of the 1980s, it was the Rams that got the 49ers' blood boiling most vigorously. First behind the running of Eric Dickerson, then the passing of Jim Everett, John Robinson's Los Angeles teams always were in the playoff hunt. New Orleans emerged as another division rival in the late 1980s and early 1990s.

In an era of NFC dominance, teams from other divisions in the conference also loomed as threats. The Bears, Redskins, and Vikings all came calling in more than one postseason show-

down. The Giants and 49ers faced off in six playoff games between 1981 and 1994, with the teams splitting the victories at three apiece.

But it was Dallas that many fans look upon as San Francisco's greatest rival during the DeBartolo years. The 49ers turned the corner by defeating the Cowboys in week 6 of the 1981 season, and ended years of postseason frustration by knocking off the Cowboys in the 1981 NFC Championship Game. Dallas returned the favor in 1992, tilting the balance of power once again. That was the first of three consecutive years in which San Francisco and Dallas met in the conference finals. They were the two best teams in football, and their showdowns were indelible.

The outcome of a 1981 49ers-Rams clash was reflected in Jack Youngblood's face: San Francisco 33, Los Angeles 31.

KEITH FAHNHORST: Our biggest rival was always the Rams....I can't remember the first time we beat 'em, but we regularly got beat by the Rams in my early years (nine consecutive times between 1976 and 1980). So when we started having some success, we really enjoyed it and appreciated it—especially going down to L.A. and beating 'em like we did. They were always in the playoff hunt, too. Those were big games.

MIKE WALTER: When I first got to the 49ers, the Rams game was still a big game. But we kind of took it to them. And it was almost kind of sad by the end. It just became another game. But it was special those first few years, the Dickerson years. And they had some great teams there for a while when Everett was playing.

BRENT JONES: Maybe this is a little arrogant, but we always felt our NFC Championship Game against the Cowboys was the Super Bowl. The AFC was the weaker conference....

It was getting a little frustrating (by 1994). We felt like we had better teams, but we didn't beat Dallas ....I would follow their whole season intently—the games, the stats, exactly how they played. I think some other guys on our team did, too, because we knew them and they knew us. I think at times we were mirror images of each other's team. And it was

When Dwight Clark made a reception in the 1981 NFC title game, he got the kind of treatment a bitter rival might expect.

A last-play field goal by Ray Wersching was all that separated the 49ers from the Rams on November 22, 1981.

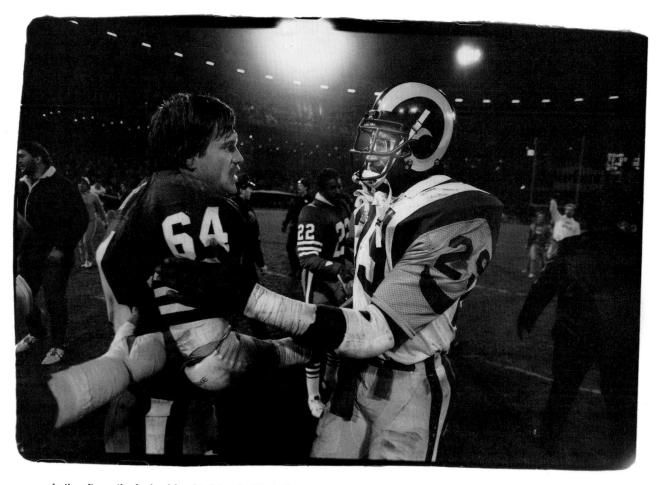

In the aftermath of a hard-fought victory in 1984, the 49ers' Jack (Hacksaw) Reynolds shook hands with Eric Dickerson.

great for football....

There's nothing that has touched it since that time. And I don't know, with the way the league works with the salary cap and the way everybody's gonna be 8-8 or 9-7 or what have you, if we'll ever see that again. It was phenomenal, and the whole football world could hardly wait for those games.

HARRIS BARTON: You look at the history of the years I was there (1987-1998). When I first got there, the Redskins were the dominant team. So that was a big rivalry. Then the Giants took over and became the big dominant team on the East Coast, and that became a big rivalry. Then, of course, the Cowboys became a big rivalry. Then

Green Bay came in and started playing real well. They became the rivalry in the NFC. So what you see is four or five different rivals come up. But what you also have is one team that's always consistent. We were always there.

JESSE SAPOLU: The Bears had a great run for maybe two or three years. The Giants challenged us for maybe four years. We played against Cincinnati in a couple of Super Bowls. But in the eighties we never heard much about the Dallas Cowboys. They were nowhere to be found—not until the nineties, when they drafted great winners like Troy Aikman, Michael Irvin, Emmitt Smith, and a core of other players who came in and said, "Hey, we're gonna turn this thing around."

But who was still there to challenge them? That was the San Francisco 49ers. That's what was special about our dynasty.

Mark Bavaro and the Giants were more than a handful on December 1, 1986, as Ronnie Lott (42) and Keena Turner discovered in a 21-17 defeat. A month later, the Giants blew the 49ers out of the playoffs in a 49-3 rout.

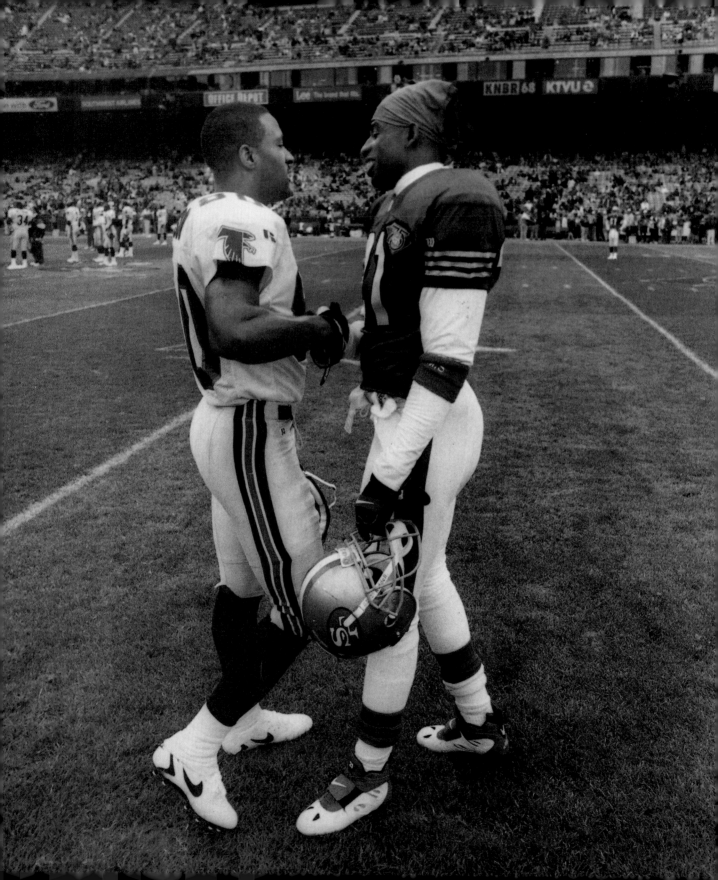

CHAPTER TWENTY-TWO

1994:
CHASING THE DEMONS

L ooking at a roster that was beginning to show its age, and frustrated after consecutive NFC title-game losses to Dallas, the 49ers undertook some renovation in 1994.

They cut ties with popular veterans such as Guy McIntyre, Tom Rathman, and Mike Walter, and welcomed a wave of new starters, including defensive end Rickey Jackson, cornerback Deion Sanders, and rookies such as fullback William Floyd and defensive tackle Bryant Young. They even poached an important member of the Cowboys, outside linebacker Ken Norton Jr. Of course, Steve Young and the incomparable Jerry Rice still were around.

After an embarrassing 40-8 home loss to Philadelphia dropped San Francisco to 3-2 in early October, the mix of talent quickly started to jell. The 49ers rattled off 10 consecutive victories, most of them runaways, before dropping a meaningless game at Minnesota to end the regular season.

The NFC Championship Game once again brought a confrontation with Dallas. This time the 49ers jumped out to a 21-0 lead midway through the first quarter and held on for a 38-28 win. Young celebrated the milestone with a manic victory lap around the Candlestick Park perimeter. Two weeks later, San Francisco buried the Chargers 49-26 in Super Bowl XXIX.

The addition of Deion Sanders (bandana) in 1994 made the 49ers' defense even more formidable.

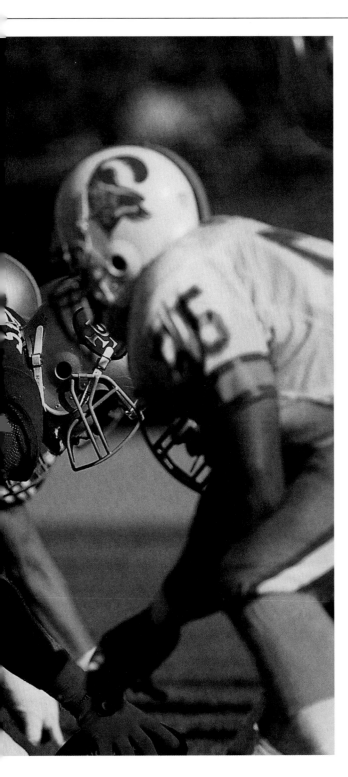

MICHAEL ZAGARIS: The big move that year was when we got Prime Time (cornerback Deion Sanders). The week before, we had lost to Kansas City. It was the Montana-Young rematch. And Steve got beat up pretty good. And then we got Prime Time and never looked back.

HARRIS BARTON: That year was special, having Deion and Rickey Jackson. We had some fierce pass rushers and some great linebackers. Ken Norton came in, and (safety) Merton Hanks (had a great season). All that stuff gets kind of lost in the offensive production of Jerry Rice and Steve Young and (running back) Ricky Watters, certainly. But that team was as good defensively as any I've been around. We knew that if we scored 7 points, we were gonna win the game.

BRENT JONES: I guess Eric Davis' interception early (in the NFC title game) is the one memory that stands out in my mind. We had already had some emotion. That was just a big turnover at home, with an electric crowd, playing against our rival in the biggest game of the year.

CARMEN POLICY: Steve's lap was a symbol of the triumph of man over adversity. Everyone felt it.

The 49ers' offense hit on all cylinders in 1994, with Steve Young setting an NFL record for passer rating.

BRENT JONES: It could have been a premature celebration, and it was very out of character for him to do that. That made it even more special, because I think it let a little bit of a window into the type of pressure he had felt.

When we prepared for the Super Bowl, we looked at the film from our regular-season game (against the Chargers, a 38-15 victory). And we thought, "There's just no way they're gonna do this and think they can beat us, and match their guys against ours (in XXIX)."

Darned if they didn't come out and do the same thing....Right off the bat everybody knew, "This is gonna be unbelievable."

CARMEN POLICY: We were fortunate enough to have five parades. That first Super Bowl, the celebration was unbelievable. But the fifth seemed to possess the same level of emotion and appreciation as the first.

The players stood united prior to a 41-16 victory over Tampa Bay,

a symbolic gesture that they repeated throughout the season.

CHAPTER TWENTY-THREE

END OF AN ERA

he 49ers remained one of the NFL's elite teams from 1995-98, winning two division titles and forging a cumulative record of 48-16 during that span. But age—and the Green Bay Packers—were catching up with the club.

The Packers, coached by former San Francisco offensive coordinator Mike Holmgren, knocked off the 49ers three consecutive years (1995-97) in the postseason. More troublesome in the long term, the team's nucleus of veteran talent began to dissolve. Many players retired (John Taylor after the 1995 season, Jesse Sapolu two seasons later), and some who remained began to show their age.

In the past, Eddie DeBartolo simply would have restocked the pond. Now the salary cap made that harder to accomplish. Then DeBartolo was gone, suspended by the league in 1997. George Seifert gave way to Steve Mariucci that year as well. Soon, two other high-ranking executives, Carmen Policy and Dwight Clark, left for the new Cleveland franchise.

The firmament was beginning to crumble, and it came down hard in 1999, when Steve Young suffered his final on-field concussion and gave way to a pair of unproven quarterbacks. The 49ers finished 4-12.

It was the moment San Francisco—the franchise, the city—had dreaded for more than 15 years. The dynasty was dead. It was painful to watch. And yet, only two years after the collapse, a new generation of 49ers was back in the playoffs. Only time will tell if they—or any other NFL team—can build an empire to match the DeBartolo years.

As long as Steve Young (left) and Jerry Rice performed at a high level, the 49ers believed they could contend for a title.

MICHAEL ZAGARIS: Even at the time, I knew this wasn't going to go on forever. Nothing is forever. Not dynasties, not ownership. But like anything else, you always wanted it to go on—for one more year. And then one more year after that.

CARMEN POLICY: We realized as early as '92, certainly in '93, when it became known that free agency and the salary cap were coming, that we would not be able to engage in business as usual. We made a business decision during troubled business times, to try one last time to build a champion. We reworked certain contracts, brought in free agents. This was probably the darkest moment for the DeBartolo Corporation financially, but we were so committed to try to win a championship.

JOHN McVAY: You've seen teams do it every year since the salary cap started in '93. Every time a team thinks it's close, like most recently Jacksonville and Washington, you say, "To hell with it. We may never get this close again. Let's go for it." Teams do that. And you say, "We'll rebuild next year, or the year after."

If you've got all the pieces in place, then you're willing to say, "Okay, let's go get a defensive end. Let's get Deion Sanders. Let's make our run at it."

But you know full well that you're gonna have to bite the bullet eventually.

As injuries and the salary cap took their toll, the 49ers' glory years began to seem like a distant memory.

ERIC WRIGHT: I don't think George was treated fairly in terms of how Dwight and Carmen rolled him out of here. It wasn't just, from the standpoint of what George had going and what those guys expected of him. That's my personal opinion.

DWIGHT CLARK: It actually was all part of a plan. Our plan was to stay competitive as long as Steve Young and Jerry Rice were able to perform at a high level.... Because we felt that as long as those two guys were playing, we had a shot at winning the Super Bowl. We knew at some point that the cap was gonna catch up with us. But the plan was to keep the team alive and be in the hunt every year until those guys either couldn't play at a high level or had decided to call their careers off. Once those two players decided it was over for 'em, then we were ready to break it down, start over, start

Not even the steadying hand of George Seifert could stem the tide when the 49ers began their descent from the top.

bringing in young guys and retooling and building it back up again.

Unfortunately, there were situations outside of the football team that caused Carmen to move on, and then eventually me to move on, before we were able to rebuild the team. I've heard some criticism about us running out after ruining the cap situation. Well, we didn't plan on leaving.

And we kept trying to plug guys in to get us back there one more time. But Dallas was too good, and then Green Bay got too good, and we just couldn't get over the hump with those two teams. When Steve started getting those concussions, it was over.

JOHN MCVAY: When I came back (in 1998), we were about $38 million over the cap. We said, "Well, let's see if we can put it together again." We said it would take us three years, and it took us three years.

You know, when I introduced Bill (Walsh) at the Hall of Fame, I mentioned it was like Camelot. I remember my speech. And you know what? It was a piece of Camelot. Those years before free agency, before franchise free agency and the salary cap, you could operate a little differently. It will never be the same. Never be the same.

—EDDIE DeBARTOLO

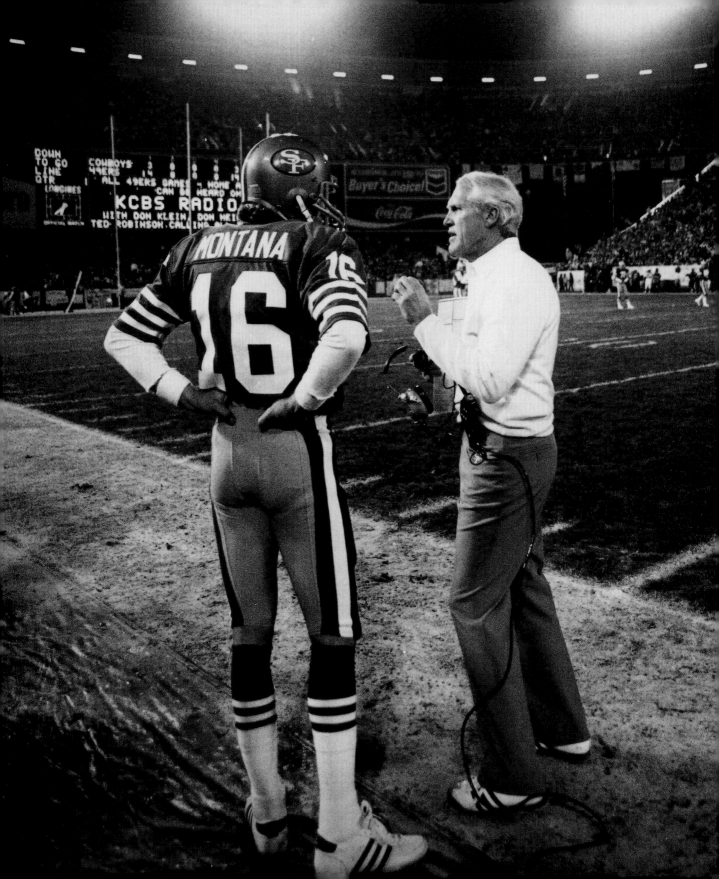

THE DYNASTY YEARS

SUPER SEASONS

Joe Montana and Bill Walsh were the catalysts for a 49ers dynasty that spanned 14 seasons.

From 1981-1994, the San Francisco 49ers were the most formidable team in the NFL. Across those 14 seasons, they compiled a record of 178-63-1 (including postseason), averaging more than 12 victories per season and recording a winning percentage of .738. First, under coach Bill Walsh (1981-88) and then under George Seifert, they made 12 playoff appearances, won 11 NFC West Division crowns, appeared in nine NFC Championship Games, and became the first team to win five Super Bowls. A recap:

1981 (16-3) FIRST PLACE, NFC WEST

Joe Montana's first full season as a starter began inauspiciously when the 49ers lost two of their first three games. But fortunes changed on September 27 with a 21-14 victory over New Orleans—the first of 15 victories in the next 16 games.

Montana blossomed in his third NFL season, passing for 19 touchdowns and 3,565 yards, and led the NFC in passer rating. Third-year receiver Dwight Clark (85 receptions, 1,105 yards) posted the only 1,000-yard receiving season of his career. A ballhawking secondary that featured Dwight Hicks and three rookies—Ronnie Lott, Carlton Williamson, and Eric Wright—accounted for 23 interceptions.

Montana and Clark wrote their names into 49ers lore when they teamed up for "The Catch" in a 28-27 victory over the Dallas Cowboys in the NFC title game. In Super Bowl XVI, the defense took center stage with a pivotal, third-quarter goal-line stand in a 26-21 victory over the Cincinnati Bengals.

L	17	at Detroit (Sept. 6)	24
W	28	Chicago (Sept. 13)	17
L	17	at Atlanta (Sept. 20)	34
W	21	New Orleans (Sept. 27)	14
W	30	at Washington (Oct. 4)	17
W	45	Dallas (Oct. 11)	14
W	13	Green Bay in Milwaukee (Oct. 18)	3
W	20	Los Angeles Rams (Oct. 25)	17
W	17	at Pittsburgh (Nov. 1)	14
W	17	Atlanta (Nov. 8)	14
L	12	Cleveland (Nov. 15)	15
W	33	at Los Angeles Rams (Nov. 22)	31
W	17	New York Giants (Nov. 29)	10
W	21	at Cincinnati (Dec. 6)	3
W	28	Houston (Dec. 13)	6
W	21	at New Orleans (Dec. 20)	17
	357		250

NFC Divisional Playoff

W	38	New York Giants (Jan. 3)	24

NFC Championship

W	28	Dallas (Jan. 10)	27

Super Bowl XVI

(at Pontiac, Michigan - Silverdome)

W	26	Cincinnati (Jan. 24)	21

1982 (3-6) ELEVENTH PLACE, NFC*

*No divisional races because of strike-shortened schedule

After beginning the season with two narrow defeats and then sitting idle for seven weeks during a players' strike, the 49ers never found the magic that had propelled them a year earlier. By the time December 19 had come and gone, the defending Super Bowl champions owned a 2-5 record and had been outscored 172-163. Even with the playoff field expanded to include 16 teams, the 49ers were left behind.

L	17	Los Angeles Raiders (Sept. 12)	23
L	21	at Denver (Sept. 19)	24
W	31	at St. Louis (Nov. 21)	20
L	20	New Orleans (Nov. 28)	23
W	30	at Los Angeles Rams (Thurs.) (Dec. 2)	24
L	37	San Diego (Sat.) (Dec. 11)	41
L	7	Atlanta (Dec. 19)	17
W	26	at Kansas City (Dec. 26)	13
L	20	Los Angeles Rams (Jan. 2)	21
	209		206

1983 (11-7) FIRST PLACE, NFC WEST

The additions of veteran Wendell Tyler and rookie Roger Craig immediately improved the 49ers' rushing attack (2,257 yards, 4.4 yards per carry), and Joe Montana enjoyed a prolific passing year (3,910 yards), thanks in part to the receiving skills of the new running backs.

Dwight Clark scored on 8 of his team-best 70 catches, and Freddie Solomon set a club record by averaging 21.4 yards per reception. An aggressive defense led by Eric Wright and Ronnie Lott pilfered 24 passes, 5 of which were returned for touchdowns.

After winning the NFC West title, the 49ers defeated the Detroit Lions in a divisional playoff game on a 14-yard touchdown pass to Solomon with 2 minutes to play. The tables were turned in the NFC Championship Game when the 49ers rallied from a 21-0 fourth-quarter deficit to tie the score only to lose to the Washington Redskins on Mark Moseley's 25-yard field goal with 40 seconds left.

L	17	Philadelphia (Sat.) (Sept. 3)	22
W	48	at Minnesota (Thurs.) (Sept. 8)	17
W	42	at St. Louis (Sept. 18)	27
W	24	Atlanta (Sept. 25)	20
W	33	at New England (Oct. 2)	13
L	7	Los Angeles Rams (Oct. 9)	10
W	32	at New Orleans (Oct. 16)	13
W	45	at Los Angeles Rams (Oct. 23)	35
L	13	New York Jets (Oct. 30)	27
L	17	Miami (Nov. 6)	20
W	27	New Orleans (Nov. 13)	0
L	24	at Atlanta (Nov. 20)	28
L	3	at Chicago (Nov. 27)	13
W	35	Tampa Bay (Dec. 4)	21
W	23	at Buffalo (Dec. 11)	10
W	42	Dallas (Mon.) (Dec. 19)	17
	432		293

NFC Divisional Playoff

W	24	Detroit (Sat.) (Dec. 31)	23

NFC Championship

L	21	at Washington (Jan. 8)	24

1984 (18-1) FIRST PLACE, NFC WEST

Only a 20-17 loss to Pittsburgh in week 7 stood between the 49ers and a perfect season. Wendell Tyler, with 1,262 yards, became the club's first 1,000-yard rusher in eight years, and Joe Montana led the NFC in passer rating (102.9) and tied for the conference lead in touchdown passes (28).

After outscoring regular-season opponents 475-227, the 49ers defeated the New York Giants (21-10) to advance to the NFC Championship Game. Then a suffocating defense (9 sacks) limited the Chicago Bears to 186 total yards in a 23-0 victory that secured a berth opposite the Miami Dolphins in Super Bowl XIX. Montana outshined the Dolphins' Dan Marino in a 38-16 victory, passing for 3 touchdowns and running for 1. He was named Super Bowl MVP.

W	30	at Detroit (Sept. 2)	27
W	37	Washington (Mon.) (Sept. 10)	31
W	30	New Orleans (Sept. 16)	20
W	21	at Philadelphia (Sept. 23)	9
W	14	Atlanta (Sept. 30)	5
W	31	at New York Giants (Mon.) (Oct. 8)	10
L	17	Pittsburgh (Oct. 14)	20
W	34	at Houston (Oct. 21)	21
W	33	at Los Angeles Rams (Oct. 28)	0
W	23	Cincinnati (Nov. 4)	17
W	41	at Cleveland (Nov. 11)	7
W	24	Tampa Bay (Nov. 18)	17
W	35	at New Orleans (Nov. 25)	3
W	35	at Atlanta (Dec. 2)	17
W	51	Minnesota (Sat.) (Dec. 8)	7
W	19	Los Angeles Rams (Fri.) (Dec. 14)	16
	475		227

NFC Divisional Playoff

W	21	New York Giants (Sat.) (Dec. 29)	10

NFC Championship

W	23	Chicago (Jan. 6)	0

Super Bowl XIX

(at Palo Alto, California - Stanford Stadium)

W	38	Miami (Jan. 20)	16

1985 (10-7) SECOND PLACE, NFC WEST

Running back Roger Craig became the first player in history to exceed 1,000 yards in both rushing and receiving, and rookie wide receiver Jerry Rice made his debut with 49 catches for 927 yards. But injuries to Joe Montana—he missed one game and parts of three others—and a revamped defense with four new starters prevented the 49ers from generating any momentum. A 10-6 record earned a wild-card playoff berth, but a 17-3 loss to the Giants in New York put an end to their postseason.

L	21	at Minnesota (Sept. 8)	28
W	35	Atlanta (Sept. 15)	16
W	34	at Los Angeles Raiders (Sept. 22)	10
L	17	New Orleans (Sept. 29)	20
W	38	at Atlanta (Oct. 6)	17
L	10	Chicago (Oct. 13)	26
L	21	at Detroit (Oct. 20)	23
W	28	at Los Angeles Rams (Oct. 27)	14
W	24	Philadelphia (Nov. 3)	13
L	16	at Denver (Mon.) (Nov. 11)	17
W	31	Kansas City (Nov. 17)	3
W	19	Seattle (Mon.) (Nov. 25)	6
W	35	at Washington (Dec. 1)	8
L	20	Los Angeles Rams (Mon.) (Dec. 9)	27
W	31	at New Orleans (Dec. 15)	19
W	31	Dallas (Dec. 22)	16
	411		263

NFC Wild Card Playoff

L	3	at New York Giants (Sat.) (Dec. 28)	17

1986 (10-6-1) FIRST PLACE, NFC WEST

Joe Montana completed 32 of 46 passes for 356 yards in a season-opening victory over the Tampa Bay Buccaneers, but the victory came at a price. A ruptured disc sent him to the sideline for eight weeks, during which Jeff Kemp led the team to a 4-3-1 record. Montana returned to direct the 49ers to five victories in seven games and a divisional title. But the postseason ended abruptly in New York, where Montana was

sent to the sideline with a second-quarter concussion and the 49ers were crushed 49-3.

W	31	at Tampa Bay (Sept. 7)	7
L	13	at Los Angeles Rams (Sept. 14)	16
W	26	New Orleans (Sept. 21)	17
W	31	at Miami (Sept. 28)	17
W	35	Indianapolis (Oct. 5)	14
L	24	Minnesota (Oct. 12)	(OT) 27
T	10	at Atlanta (Oct. 19)	(OT) 10
W	31	Green Bay in Milwaukee (Oct. 26)	17
L	10	at New Orleans (Nov. 2)	23
W	43	St. Louis (Nov. 9)	17
L	6	at Washington (Mon.) (Nov. 17)	14
W	20	Atlanta (Nov. 23)	0
L	17	New York Giants (Mon.) (Dec. 1)	21
W	24	New York Jets (Dec. 7)	10
W	29	at New England (Dec. 14)	24
W	24	Los Angeles Rams (Fri.) (Dec. 19)	14
	374		247

NFC Divisional Playoff

L	3	at New York Giants (Jan. 4)	49

1987 (13-3) FIRST PLACE, NFC WEST

The 49ers swept through the regular season with barely a hitch, losing only the opener at Pittsburgh (30-17) and in game 9 to the New Orleans Saints (26-24).

Despite two games lost to injury and one to a players' strike, Joe Montana passed for a club-record 31 touchdowns. Jerry Rice, in his third season, accounted for 1,078 receiving yards and an NFL-record 22 scoring catches. Steve Young, in his first year with the club, came off the bench to pass for 10 touchdowns in just 69 attempts.

The steamroller came to a screeching halt in a stunning 36-24 divisional playoff loss to the Minnesota Vikings, owners of an 8-7 regular-season record. Vikings wide receiver Anthony Carter caught 10 passes for a postseason-record 227 yards. Montana ended the game on the bench, removed in favor of Young.

L	17	at Pittsburgh (Sept. 13)	30
W	27	at Cincinnati (Sept. 20)	26
		*Philadelphia	
W	41	at New York Giants (Mon.) (Oct. 5)	21
W	25	at Atlanta (Oct. 11)	17
W	34	St. Louis (Oct. 18)	28
W	24	at New Orleans (Oct. 25)	22
W	31	at Los Angeles Rams (Nov. 1)	10
W	27	Houston (Nov. 8)	20
L	24	New Orleans (Nov. 15)	26
W	24	at Tampa Bay (Nov. 22)	10
W	38	Cleveland (Nov. 29)	24
W	23	at Green Bay (Dec. 6)	12
W	41	Chicago (Mon.) (Dec. 14)	0
W	35	Atlanta (Dec. 20)	7
W	48	Los Angeles Rams (Dec. 27)	0
	459		253

NFC Divisional Playoff

L	24	Minnesota (Sat.) (Jan. 9)	36

* Game canceled because of NFL players' strike.

1988 (13-6) FIRST PLACE, NFC WEST

The 49ers seemed headed nowhere when they owned a 6-5 record with five games left in the season. Among the teams they had lost to were the Falcons, Broncos, Cardinals, and Raiders, none of which were en route to a winning season. But a sudden burst—four victories in five games—enabled San Francisco to compile a 10-6 record and, thanks to a tie breaker, edge out the Rams for the divisional title.

Once the postseason arrived, the 49ers caught fire. A 34-9 divisional victory over Minnesota, in which Joe Montana threw 3 touchdown passes to Jerry Rice, avenged an upset loss from the previous season. A 28-3 victory over the Chicago Bears in the NFC title game featured 2 more touchdown passes from Montana to Rice. Finally, in Super Bowl XXIII, Montana capped the season with a 92-yard touchdown drive that ended with a game-winning pass to John Taylor with 34 seconds to play.

W	34	at New Orleans (Sept. 4)	33
W	20	at New York Giants (Sept. 11)	17
L	17	Atlanta (Sept. 18)	34
W	38	at Seattle (Sept. 25)	7
W	20	Detroit (Oct. 2)	13
L	13	Denver (Oct. 9) (OT)	16
W	24	at Los Angeles Rams (Oct. 16)	21
L	9	at Chicago (Mon.) (Oct. 24)	10
W	24	Minnesota (Oct. 30)	21
L	23	at Phoenix (Nov. 6)	24
L	3	Los Angeles Raiders (Nov. 13)	9
W	37	Washington (Mon.) (Nov. 21)	21
W	48	at San Diego (Nov. 27)	10
W	13	at Atlanta (Dec. 4)	3
W	30	New Orleans (Dec. 11)	17
L	16	Los Angeles Rams (Dec. 18)	38
	369		294

NFC Divisional Playoff

W	34	Minnesota (Jan. 1)	9

NFC Championship

W	28	at Chicago (Jan. 8)	3

Super Bowl XXIII

(at Miami - Joe Robbie Stadium)

W	20	Cincinnati (Jan. 22)	16

1989 (17-2) FIRST PLACE, NFC WEST

Only twice all season did the 49ers fail to score at least 20 points, and those were the only two games they lost—13-12 to the Rams and 21-17 to the Packers. Jerry Rice (1,483 yards, 17 touchdowns) and John Taylor (1,077, 10) were an unstoppable combination at wide receiver, and Roger Craig (1,054 yards) provided the ground attack. Joe Montana, for the second time in his career, led the NFL in passer rating (a league-record 112.4).

Under new coach George Seifert, the 49ers especially excelled in the postseason, winning their final three games by margins of 28, 27, and 45 points. Montana passed for 4 touchdowns, and Craig rushed for 118 yards in a 41-13 victory over the Vikings. One week later, the 49ers intercepted Jim Everett 3 times, and Montana completed 26 of 30 passes in a 30-3 victory over the Rams in the NFC Championship Game.

In Super Bowl XXIV, the 49ers exploded for a 55-10 victory over the Broncos. Montana passed for a record 5 touchdowns and was selected the game's MVP for an unprecedented third time.

W	30	at Indianapolis (Sept. 10)	24
W	20	at Tampa Bay (Sept. 17)	16
W	38	at Philadelphia (Sept. 24)	28
L	12	Los Angeles Rams (Oct. 1)	13
W	24	at New Orleans (Oct. 8)	20
W	31	at Dallas (Oct. 15)	14
W	37	†New England (Oct. 22)	20
W	23	at New York Jets (Oct. 29)	10
W	31	New Orleans (Mon.) (Nov. 6)	13
W	45	Atlanta (Nov. 12)	3
L	17	Green Bay (Nov. 19)	21
W	34	New York Giants (Mon.) (Nov. 27)	24
W	23	at Atlanta (Dec. 3)	10
W	30	at Los Angeles Rams (Mon.) (Dec. 11)	27
W	21	Buffalo (Dec. 17)	10
W	26	Chicago (Dec. 24)	0
	442		253

NFC Divisional Playoff

W	41	Minnesota (Sat.) (Jan. 6)	13

NFC Championship

W	30	Los Angeles Rams (Jan. 14)	3

Super Bowl XXIV

(at New Orleans - Louisiana Superdome)

W	55	Denver (Jan. 28)	10

† Game played at Stanford Stadium because of Bay Area earthquake

1990 (15-3) FIRST PLACE, NFC WEST

The 49ers and the Giants, each of which won their first 10 games, were headed on a collision course almost from the moment the season began. Their first collision came in week 13 on a Monday night in San Francisco, where Joe Montana's 4-yard touchdown pass to John Taylor held up for a 7-3 victory. The second collision came in the NFC Championship Game, in which the 49ers owned a 13-12 lead late in the fourth quarter.

The tide turned with 2:36 left to play when the Giants' Lawrence Taylor recovered Roger Craig's fumble at New York's 43-yard line. The Giants marched to the 49ers' 25 and, as time expired, Matt Bahr converted a 42-yard field goal that sent New York to Super Bowl XXV.

W	13	at New Orleans (Mon.) (Sept. 10)	12
W	26	Washington (Sept. 16)	13
W	19	Atlanta (Sept. 23)	13
		BYE	
W	24	at Houston (Oct. 7)	21
W	45	at Atlanta (Oct. 14)	35
W	27	Pittsburgh (Oct. 21)	7
W	20	Cleveland (Oct. 28)	17
W	24	at Green Bay (Nov. 4)	20
W	24	at Dallas (Nov. 11)	6
W	31	Tampa Bay (Nov. 18)	7
L	17	Los Angeles Rams (Nov. 25)	28
W	7	New York Giants (Mon.) (Dec. 3)	3
W	20	at Cincinnati (Dec. 9) (OT)	17
W	26	at Los Angeles Rams (Mon.) (Dec. 17)	10
L	10	New Orleans (Dec. 23)	13
W	20	at Minnesota (Dec. 30)	17
	353		239

NFC Divisional Playoff

W	28	Washington (Sat.) (Jan. 12)	10

NFC Championship

L	13	New York Giants (Jan. 20)	15

1991 (10-6) THIRD PLACE, NFC WEST

With Joe Montana sidelined for the season because of a torn tendon in his right elbow and Steve Young knocked out with a knee injury in week 10, the 49ers struggled on and off the field throughout the season. The team finally jelled under third-string quarterback Steve Bono, winning its last six games. But the 49ers were edged out for a wild-card playoff berth by the Falcons on a tie breaker.

L	14	at New York Giants (Mon.) (Sept. 2)	16
W	34	San Diego (Sept. 8)	14
L	14	at Minnesota (Sept. 15)	17
W	27	Los Angeles Rams (Sept. 22)	10
L	6	at Los Angeles Raiders (Sept. 29)	12
		BYE	
L	34	Atlanta (Oct. 13)	39
W	35	Detroit (Oct. 20)	3
W	23	at Philadelphia (Oct. 27)	7
L	14	at Atlanta (Nov. 3)	17
L	3	at New Orleans (Nov. 10)	10
W	14	Phoenix (Nov. 17)	10
W	33	at Los Angeles Rams (Mon.) (Nov. 25)	10
W	38	New Orleans (Dec. 1)	24
W	24	at Seattle (Dec. 8)	22
W	28	Kansas City (Sat.) (Dec. 14)	14
W	52	Chicago (Mon.) (Dec. 22)	14
	393		239

1992 (15-3) FIRST PLACE, NFC WEST

With Joe Montana still ailing, Steve Young claimed the starting quarterback job as his own, passing for 3,465 yards and leading the NFL in passer rating. Jerry Rice was his favorite target, with 84 receptions for 1,201 yards and 10 touchdowns. Second-year back Ricky Watters, who missed his entire rookie season with a foot injury, rushed for 1,013 yards and 9 touchdowns.

The 49ers were unbeaten within their division, easily claiming the NFC West crown and earning home-field advantage throughout the playoffs. After a 20-13 divisional playoff victory over the Redskins, in which Young passed for 227 yards and rushed for 73, the 49ers collided with Dallas in the first of three successive NFC title-game meetings. The Cowboys won 30-20, thanks to 4 turnovers by the 49ers and the arm of Troy Aikman, who passed for 322 yards and 2 touchdowns.

W	31	at New York Giants (Sept. 6)	14
L	31	Buffalo (Sept. 13)	34
W	31	at New York Jets (Sept. 20)	14
W	16	at New Orleans (Sept. 27)	10
W	27	Los Angeles Rams (Oct. 4)	24
W	24	at New England (Oct. 11)	12
W	56	Atlanta (Oct. 18)	17
		BYE	
L	14	at Phoenix (Nov. 1)	24
W	41	at Atlanta (Mon.) (Nov. 9)	3
W	21	New Orleans (Nov. 15)	20
W	27	at Los Angeles Rams (Nov. 22)	10
W	20	Philadelphia (Nov. 29)	14
W	27	Miami (Dec. 6)	3
W	20	at Minnesota (Dec. 13)	17
W	21	Tampa Bay (Dec. 19)	14
W	24	Detroit (Mon.) (Dec. 28)	6
	431		236
NFC Divisional Playoff			
W	20	Washington (Sat.) (Jan. 9)	13
NFC Championship			
L	20	Dallas (Jan. 17)	30

1993 (11-7) FIRST PLACE, NFC WEST

An offseason trade sent Joe Montana to Kansas City and placed the 49ers' fortunes unquestionably in Steve Young's hands. He responded with 4,023 passing yards, 29 touchdown passes, and another NFL passing title. Ricky Watters picked up where he had left off in 1992, rushing for 950 yards and 10 touchdowns.

After a rocky start—they were 3-3 after six games—the 49ers regained their stride to win six consecutive games en route to their seventh NFC West title in eight seasons. They blew away the New York Giants 44-3 in a divisional playoff game but then were forced to travel to Dallas in the NFC title game. The Cowboys raced to a 28-7 halftime lead, before settling for a 38-21 victory and a second consecutive Super Bowl appearance.

W	24	at Pittsburgh (Sept. 5)	13
L	13	at Cleveland (Mon.) (Sept. 13)	23
W	37	Atlanta (Sept. 19)	30
L	13	at New Orleans (Sept. 26)	16
W	38	Minnesota (Oct. 3)	19
		BYE	
L	17	at Dallas (Oct. 17)	26
W	28	Phoenix (Oct. 24)	14
W	40	Los Angeles Rams (Oct. 31)	17
		BYE	
W	45	at Tampa Bay (Nov. 14)	21
W	42	New Orleans (Mon.) (Nov. 22)	7
W	35	at Los Angeles Rams (Nov. 28)	10
W	21	Cincinnati (Dec. 5)	8
L	24	at Atlanta (Sat.) (Dec. 11)	27
W	55	at Detroit (Dec. 19)	17

L	7	Houston (Sat.) (Dec. 25)	10
L	34	Philadelphia (Mon.) (Jan. 3)	(OT) 37
	473		295
NFC Divisional Playoff			
W	44	New York Giants (Jan. 15)	3
NFC Championship			
L	21	at Dallas (Jan. 23)	38

1994 (16-3) FIRST PLACE, NFC WEST

One of the most explosive teams in 49ers history—they led the league in scoring with 505 points—recorded blowout upon blowout during a 13-3 regular season. Steve Young enjoyed the finest statistical season of his career, setting an NFL record with a 112.8 passer rating to claim his fourth consecutive passing title. Jerry Rice had 112 receptions, the highest total in his first 10 seasons. Rookie William Floyd joined Ricky Watters in the backfield, and together they rushed for 12 touchdowns. The defense benefited from the arrival of free-agent cornerback Deion Sanders, who returned 3 of his 6 interceptions for touchdowns.

After claiming home-field advantage throughout the playoffs, the 49ers disposed of the Chicago Bears 44-15 in a divisional playoff game and braced for the Cowboys in the NFC Championship Game. Three first-quarter touchdowns—on a 44-yard interception return by Eric Davis, a 29-yard pass to Watters, and a 1-yard run by Floyd—sent the 49ers on their way to a 38-28 victory. Young passed for a record 6 touchdowns in his only Super Bowl start, as the 49ers defeated the San Diego Chargers 49-26.

W	44	Los Angeles Raiders (Mon.) (Sat. 5)	14
L	17	at Kansas City (Sept. 11)	24
W	34	at Los Angeles Rams (Sept. 18)	19
W	24	New Orleans (Sept. 25)	13
L	8	Philadelphia (Oct. 2)	40
W	27	at Detroit (Oct. 9)	21
W	42	at Atlanta (Oct. 16)	3
W	41	Tampa Bay (Oct. 23)	16
		BYE	
W	37	at Washington (Nov. 6)	22
W	21	Dallas (Nov. 13)	14
W	31	Los Angeles Rams (Nov. 20)	27
W	35	at New Orleans (Mon.) (Nov. 28)	14
W	50	Atlanta (Dec. 4)	14
W	38	at San Diego (Sat.) (Dec. 11)	15
W	42	Denver (Sat.) (Dec. 18)	19
L	14	at Minnesota (Mon.) (Dec. 26)	21
	505		296
NFC Divisional Playoff			
W	44	Chicago (Sat.) (Jan. 7)	15
NFC Championship			
W	38	Dallas (Jan. 15)	28
Super Bowl XXIX			
		(at Miami - Joe Robbie Stadium)	
W	49	San Diego (Jan. 29)	26

Subsequent 49ers Super Bowl teams would be accorded more acclaim, but none was more opportunistic than the champions of game XVI. They scored their first touchdown after Dwight Hicks made an interception in the shadow of his goal post. They scored a second after Lynn Thomas recovered a Bengals fumble at the 49ers' 8-yard line. They added a field goal just before halftime when Cincinnati fumbled a kickoff return. Just that quickly, the 49ers raced ahead 20-0. Holding on to the lead was something else

again. The pivotal series in a second half that belonged to Cincinnati came late in the third quarter when the Bengals, trailing 20-7, owned a first-and-goal at the 49ers' 3.

Two runs by Pete Johnson netted 2 yards, a pass to Charles Alexander was stopped for no gain, and on fourth-and-goal Johnson was stuffed at the line of scrimmage. The last 2 of Ray Wersching's 4 field goals supplied enough cushion to secure a 49ers victory on a day when they were outgained but not outplayed.

STARTING LINEUPS

San Francisco (NFC)	Offense	Cincinnati (AFC)
Dwight Clark	WR	Cris Collinsworth
Dan Audick	LT	Anthony Muñoz
John Ayers	LG	Dave Lapham
Fred Quillan	C	Blair Bush
Randy Cross	RG	Max Montoya
Keith Fahnhorst	RT	Mike Wilson
Charle Young	TE	Dan Ross
Freddie Solomon	WR	Isaac Curtis
Joe Montana	QB	Ken Anderson
Ricky Patton	RB	Charles Alexander
Earl Cooper	RB	Pete Johnson
	Defense	
Jim Stuckey	LE	Eddie Edwards
Archie Reese	NT	Wilson Whitley
Fred Dean	DT–RE	Ross Browner
Dwaine Board	DE–LOLB	Bo Harris
Bobby Leopold	LLB–LILB	Jim LeClair
Jack Reynolds	MLB–RILB	Glenn Cameron
Keena Turner	RLB–ROLB	Reggie Williams
Ronnie Lott	LCB	Louis Breeden
Eric Wright	RCB	Ken Riley
Carlton Williamson	SS	Bobby Kemp
Dwight Hicks	FS	Bryan Hicks

SUBSTITUTIONS

San Francisco–Offense: K–Ray Wersching. P–Jim Miller. RB–Johnny Davis, Amos Lawrence, Bill Ring. WR–Mike Shumann, Mike Wilson. TE–Eason Ramson. C–Walt Downing. T–Allan Kennedy. G–John Choma. **Defense:** DE–Lawrence Pillers. DT–John Harty. LB–Dan Bunz, Willie Harper, Milt McColl, Craig Puki. DB–Rick Gervais, Lynn Thomas. DNP: QB–Guy Benjamin. RB–Walt Easley, Lenvil Elliott. DB–Saladin Martin.

Cincinnati–Offense: K–Jim Breech. P–Pat McInally. RB–Archie Griffin, Jim Hargrove. WR–Don Bass, Steve Kreider, David Verser. TE–M.L. Harris. C–Blake Moore. T–Mike Obrovac. **Defense:** DE–Gary Burley, Mike St. Clair. NT–Rod Horn. LB–Tom Dinkel, Guy Frazier, Rick Razzano. DB–Oliver Davis, Mike Fuller, Ray Griffin, John Simmons. DNP: QB–Turk Schonert, Jack Thompson. G–Glenn Bujnoch.

SCORING

San Francisco	7	13	0	6	—	26
Cincinnati	0	0	7	14	—	21

SF–Montana 1 run (Wersching kick)
SF–Cooper 11 pass from Montana (Wersching kick)
SF–FG Wersching 22
SF–FG Wersching 26
Cin–Anderson 5 run (Breech kick)
Cin–Ross 4 pass from Anderson (Breech kick)
SF–FG Wersching 40
SF–FG Wersching 23
Cin–Ross 3 pass from Anderson (Breech kick)
Attendance–81,270

FINAL TEAM STATISTICS

	49ers	Bengals
TOTAL FIRST DOWNS	20	24
Rushing	9	7
Passing	9	13
Penalty	2	4
TOTAL NET YARDAGE	275	356
Total Offensive Plays	63	63
Average Gain per Offensive Play	4.4	5.7
NET YARDS RUSHING	127	72
Total Rushing Plays	40	24
Average Gain per Rushing Play	3.2	3.0
NET YARDS PASSING	148	284
Pass Att.–Comp.–Int.	22–14–0	34–25–2
Times Sacked–Yards Lost	1–9	5–16
Gross Yards Passing	157	300
Avg. Gain per Pass (Incl. Sacks)	6.4	7.3
PUNTS–YARDS	4–185	3–131
Average Distance	46.3	43.7
Had Blocked	0	0
TOTAL RETURN YARDAGE	98	87
Kickoff Return–Yards	2–40	7–52
Punt Returns–Yards	1–6	4–35
Interception Returns–Yards	2–52	0–0
TOTAL TURNOVERS	1	4
Fumbles–Lost	2–1	2–2
Had Intercepted	0	2
PENALTIES–YARDS	8–65	8–57
TOTAL POINTS SCORED	26	21
Touchdowns Rushing	1	1
Touchdowns Passing	1	2
Touchdowns Returns	0	0
Extra Points	2	3
Field Goals–Attempts	4–4	0–0
Safeties	0	0
THIRD–DOWN EFFICIENCY	8/15	6/12
FOURTH–DOWN EFFICIENCY	0/0	1/2
TIME OF POSSESSION	32:13	27:47

INDIVIDUAL STATISTICS

RUSHING

San Francisco	No.	Yds.	Avg.	Long	TD
Patton	17	55	3.2	10	0
Cooper	9	34	3.8	14	0
Montana	6	18	3.0	7	1
Ring	5	17	3.4	7	0
Davis	2	5	2.5	4	0
Clark	1	–2	–2.0	–2	0
Cincinnati					
Johnson	14	36	2.6	5	0
Alexander	5	17	3.4	13	0
Anderson	4	15	3.8	6	1
A. Griffin	1	4	4.0	4	0

PASSING

San Francisco	Att.	Comp.	Yds.	Long	TD	Int.
Montana	22	14	157	22	1	0
Cincinnati						
Anderson	34	25	300	49	2	2

RECEIVING

San Francisco	No.	Yds.	Long	TD
Solomon	4	52	20	0
Clark	4	45	17	0
Cooper	2	15	11t	1
Wilson	1	22	22	0
Young	1	14	14	0
Patton	1	6	6	0
Ring	1	3	3	0
Cincinnati				
Ross	11	104	16	2
Collinsworth	5	107	49	0
Curtis	3	42	21	0
Kreider	2	36	19	0
Johnson	2	8	5	0
Alexander	2	3	3	0

PUNTING

San Francisco	No.	Yds.	Avg.	TB	Long
Miller	4	185	46.3	0	50
Cincinnati					
McInally	3	131	43.7	0	53

PUNT RETURNS

San Francisco	No.	FC	Yds.	Long	TD
Hicks	1	0	6	6	0
Solomon	0	1	0	0	0
Cincinnati					
Fuller	4	0	35	17	0

KICKOFF RETURNS

San Francisco	No.	Yds.	Long	TD
Hicks	1	23	23	0
Lawrence	1	17	17	0
Cincinnati				
Verser	5	52	16	0
Frazier	1	0	0	0
A. Griffin	1	0	0	0

RUSHING	Att.	Yds	Avg.	LG	TD
Patton, Ricky	152	543	3.6	28	4
Cooper, Earl	98	330	3.4	23	1
Davis, Johnny	94	297	3.2	14	7
Easley, Walt	76	224	3.0	9	1
Hofer, Paul	60	193	3.2	12	1
Ring, Bill	22	106	4.8	16	0
Montana, Joe	25	95	3.8	20	2
Lawrence, Amos	13	48	3.7	14	1
Solomon, Freddie	9	43	4.8	16	0
Clark, Dwight	3	32	10.7	18	0
Elliott, Lenvil	7	29	4.1	9	0
Benjamin, Guy	1	1	1.0	1	0
49ers	560	1941	3.5	28	17
OPPONENTS	464	1918	4.1	29	10

RECEIVING	No.	Yds	Avg.	LG	TD
Clark, Dwight	85	1,105	13.0	78t	4
Solomon, Freddie	59	969	16.4	60t	8
Cooper, Earl	51	477	9.4	50	0
Young, Charle	37	400	10.8	29	5
Hofer, Paul	27	244	9.0	22	0
Patton, Ricky	27	195	7.2	31	1
Wilson, Michael	9	125	13.9	27t	1
Easley, Walt	9	62	6.9	21	0
Elliott, Lenvil	7	81	11.6	19	0
Ramson, Eason	4	45	11.3	16	0
Ring, Bill	3	28	9.3	21	1
Shumann, Mike	3	21	7.0	8	0
Lawrence, Amos	3	10	3.3	5	0
Davis, Johnny	3	-1	-0.3	3	0
Peets, Brian	1	5	5.0	5	0
49ers	328	3,766	11.5	78t	20
OPPONENTS	273	3,135	11.5	67	16

INTERCEPTIONS	No.	Yds	Avg.	LG	TD
Hicks, Dwight	9	239	26.6	72	1
Lott, Ronnie	7	117	16.7	41t	3
Williamson, Carlton	4	44	11.0	28	0
Wright, Eric	3	26	8.7	26	0
McColl, Milt	1	22	22.0	22	0
Reynolds, Jack	1	0	0.0	0	0
Martin, Saladin	1	0	0.0	0	0
Turner, Keena	1	0	0.0	0	0
49ers	27	448	16.6	72	4
OPPONENTS	13	297	22.9	101t	2

KICKOFF RETURNS	No.	Yds	Avg.	LG	TD
Lawrence, Amos	17	437	25.7	92t	1
Ring, Bill	10	217	21.7	29	0
Lott, Ronnie	7	111	15.9	20	0
Wilson, Mike	4	67	16.8	22	0
Jones, Arrington	3	43	14.3	22	0
Hicks, Dwight	1	22	22.0	22	0
Ramson, Eason	1	12	12.0	12	0
Patton, Ricky	1	0	0.0	0	0
Davis, Johnny	1	0	0.0	0	0
49ers	45	909	20.2	92t	1
OPPONENTS	67	1,389	20.7	55	0

PUNT RETURNS	No.	FC	Yds	Avg.	LG	TD
Solomon, Freddie	29	6	173	6.0	19	0
Hicks, Dwight	19	4	171	9.0	39	0
49ers	48	10	344	7.2	39	0
OPPONENTS	57	8	664	11.7	58t	1

PUNTING	No.	Yds	Avg.	TB	I-20	LG	Blk
Miller, Jim	93	3,858	41.5	15	14	65	0
49ers	93	3,858	41.5	15	14	65	0
OPPONENTS	83	3,433	41.4	5	17	66	0

SCORING	TD	PAT	FG	S	PTS
Wersching, Ray	0	30/30	17/23	0	81
Solomon, Freddie	8	0/0	0/0	0	48
Davis, Johnny	7	0/0	0/0	0	42
Patton, Ricky	5	0/0	0/0	0	30
Young, Charle	5	0/0	0/0	0	30
Clark, Dwight	4	0/0	0/0	0	24
Bahr, Matt	0	12/12	2/6	0	18
Lott, Ronnie	3	0/0	0/0	0	18
Hicks, Dwight	2	0/0	0/0	0	12
Lawrence, Amos	2	0/0	0/0	0	12
Montana, Joe	2	0/0	0/0	0	12
Cooper, Earl	1	0/0	0/0	0	6
Easley, Walt	1	0/0	0/0	0	6
Hofer, Paul	1	0/0	0/0	0	6
Ring, Bill	1	0/0	0/0	0	6
Wilson, Mike	1	0/0	0/0	0	6
49ers	43	42/42	19/29	0	357
OPPONENTS	30	29/30	13/23	0	250

PASSING	Att.	Comp.	Pct.	Yds	LG	TD	Int	QB
Montana, Joe	488	311	63.7	3,565	78t	19	12	88.4
Benjamin, Guy	26	15	57.7	171	27	1	1	74.4
Easley, Walt	1	1	100.0	5	5	0	0	87.5
Solomon, Freddie	1	1	100.0	25	25	0	0	118.8
Clark, Dwight	1	0	0.0	0	0	0	0	39.6
49ers	517	328	63.4	3,766	78t	20	13	87.7
OPPONENTS	514	273	53.1	3,135	67	16	27	60.2

Rookies indicated in italic

1981 TEAM STATISTICS

	49ers	Opp.
TOTAL FIRST DOWNS	317	280
By Rushing	110	113
By Passing	183	144
By Penalties	24	23
TOTAL YARDS GAINED	5,484	4,763
By Rushing	1,941	1,918
By Passing	3,543	2,845
TOTAL PLAYS		
FROM SCRIMMAGE	1,106	1,014
Rushes	560	464
Average Gain Per Rush	3.5	4.1

	49ers	Opp.
NET YARDS PASSING	3,543	2,845
Passes Attempted	517	514
Passes Completed	328	273
Percent Completed	63.4	53.1
Had Intercepted	13	27
Times Sacked	29	36
Lost Attempting to Pass	223	290
PUNTS	93	83
Total Yardage of Punts	3,858	3,433
Average Length	41.5	41.4
KICKOFFS	45	67
Total Yards Returned	909	1,389
Average Length of Return	20.2	20.7

	49ers	Opp.
PENALTIES	92	108
Yards Penalized	752	866
FUMBLES	26	36
Own Fumbles Recovered	14	15
Oppnts' Fumbles Recovered	21	12
FIELD GOALS	19	13
Field Goals Attempted	29	23
TOTAL POINTS SCORED	357	250
Touchdowns Scored	43	30
Touchdowns Rushing	17	10
Touchdowns Passing	20	16
Touchdown Returns	6	4
Extra Points	42	29
Safeties	0	1

The 1984 49ers were one of the best teams the NFL has produced, as evidenced by a 15-1 regular-season record and two comfortable victories in the NFC playoffs. But they arrived at Super Bowl XIX in the shadow of the Miami Dolphins, whose wunderkind quarterback Dan Marino had passed for an NFL-record 48 touchdowns that season. That snub served only to inspire the 49ers' Joe Montana, who carved out a quarterbacking masterpiece in his second appearance in the big game. He completed 24 of

35 passes for 331 yards and 3 touchdowns. He also ran 5 times for 59 yards and another touchdown. By halftime, the 49ers led 28-16. By the end of the third quarter, they owned a 38-16 margin that would hold up as the final score. The 49ers owned advantages in rushing yardage, passing yardage, first downs, total plays, and time of possession, facts that did not go unnoticed by Montana: "All week, it was Miami, Miami, Miami every time we turned around. You people were overlooking us."

STARTING LINEUPS

Miami (AFC)	Offense	San Francisco (NFC)
Mark Duper	WR	Dwight Clark
Jon Giesler	LT	Bubba Paris
Roy Foster	LG	John Ayers
Dwight Stephenson	C	Fred Quillan
Ed Newman	RG	Randy Cross
Cleveland Green	RT	Keith Fahnhorst
Bruce Hardy	TE	Russ Francis
Mark Clayton	WR	Freddie Solomon
Dan Marino	QB	Joe Montana
Tony Nathan	RB	Wendell Tyler
Woody Bennett	RB	Roger Craig
	Defense	
Doug Betters	LE	Lawrence Pillers
Bob Baumhower	NT	Manu Tuiasosopo
Kim Bokamper	RE	Dwaine Board
Bob Brudzinski	LOLB	Dan Bunz
Jay Brophy	LILB	Riki Ellison
Mark Brown	RILB	Jack Reynolds
Charles Bowser	ROLB	Keena Turner
Don McNeal	LCB	Ronnie Lott
William Judson	RCB	Eric Wright
Glenn Blackwood	SS	Carlton Williamson
Lyle Blackwood	FS	Dwight Hicks

SUBSTITUTIONS

Miami–Offense: K–Uwe von Schamann. P–Reggie Roby. QB–Don Strock. RB–Joe Carter, Eddie Hill. TE–Dan Johnson, Joe Rose. WR–Jimmy Cefalo, Vince Heflin, Jim Jensen, Nat Moore. KR–Fulton Walker. G–Steve Clark, Ronnie Lee, Jeff Toews. **Defense:** DE–Bill Barnett, Charles Benson. DT–Mike Charles. LB–A.J. Duhe, Earnest Rhone, Jackie Shipp, Sanders Shiver. CB–Paul Lankford, Robert Sowell. S–Bud Brown, Mike Kozlowski. **DNP:** FB–Pete Johnson.

San Francisco–Offense: K–Ray Wersching. P–Max Runager. RB–Derrick Harmon, Carl Monroe, Bill Ring. TE–Earl Cooper. WR–Renaldo Nehemiah, Mike Wilson. KR–Dana McLemore. T–Allan Kennedy, Billy Shields. G–Guy McIntyre. **Defense:** DE–Fred Dean, Jim Stuckey. DT–Michael Carter, Gary Johnson, Louie Kelcher, Jeff Stover. LB–Milt McColl, Blanchard Montgomery, Todd Shell, Michael Walter. CB–Tom Holmoe. S–Jeff Fuller. **DNP:** QB–Matt Cavanaugh. TE–John Frank. CB–Mario Clark.

SCORING

Miami	10	6	0	0	—	16
San Francisco	7	21	10	0	—	38

Mia–FG von Schamann 37
SF–Monroe 33 pass from Montana (Wersching kick)
Mia–D. Johnson 2 pass from Marino (von Schamann kick)
SF–Craig 8 pass from Montana (Wersching kick)
SF–Montana 6 run (Wersching kick)
SF–Craig 2 run (Wersching kick)
Mia–FG von Schamann 31
Mia–FG von Schamann 30
SF–FG Wersching 27
SF–Craig 16 pass from Montana (Wersching kick)
Attendance–84,059

FINAL TEAM STATISTICS

	Dolphins	49ers
TOTAL FIRST DOWNS	19	31
Rushing	2	16
Passing	17	15
Penalty	0	0
TOTAL NET YARDAGE	314	537
Total Offensive Plays	63	76
Average Gain per Offensive Play	5.0	7.1
NET YARDS RUSHING	25	211
Total Rushing Plays	9	40
Average Gain per Rushing Play	2.8	5.3
NET YARDS PASSING	289	326
Pass Att.–Comp.–Int.	50–29–2	35–24–0
Times Sacked–Yards Lost	4–29	1–5
Gross Yards Passing	318	331
Avg. Gain per Pass (Incl. Sacks)	5.4	9.1
PUNTS–YARDS	6–236	3–98
Average Distance	39.3	32.7
Had Blocked	0	0
TOTAL RETURN YARDAGE	155	91
Kickoff Returns–Yards	7–140	4–40
Punt Returns–Yards	2–15	5–51
Interception Returns–Yards	0–0	2–0
TOTAL TURNOVERS	2	2
Fumbles–Lost	1–0	2–2
Had Intercepted	2	0
PENALTIES–YARDS	1–10	2–10
TOTAL POINTS SCORED	16	38
Touchdowns Rushing	0	2
Touchdowns Passing	1	3
Touchdowns Returns	0	0
Extra Points	1	5
Field Goals–Attempts	3–3	1–1
Safeties	0	0
THIRD–DOWN EFFICIENCY	4/12	6/11
FOURTH–DOWN EFFICIENCY	0/0	0/1
TIME OF POSSESSION	22:49	37:11

INDIVIDUAL STATISTICS

RUSHING

Miami	No.	Yds.	Avg.	Long	TD
Nathan	5	18	3.6	16	0
Bennett	3	7	2.3	7	0
Marino	1	0	0.0	0	0
San Francisco					
Tyler	13	65	5.0	9	0
Montana	5	59	11.8	19	1
Craig	15	58	3.9	10	1
Harmon	5	20	4.0	7	0
Solomon	1	5	5.0	5	0
Cooper	1	4	4.0	4	0

PASSING

Miami	Att.	Comp.	Yds.	Long	TD	Int.
Marino	50	29	318	30	1	2
San Francisco						
Montana	35	24	331	40	3	0

RECEIVING

Miami	No.	Yds.	Long	TD
Nathan	10	83	25	0
Clayton	6	92	27	0
Rose	6	73	30	0
D. Johnson	3	28	21	1
Moore	2	17	9	0
Cefalo	1	14	14	0
Duper	1	11	11	0
San Francisco				
Craig	7	77	20	2
D. Clark	6	77	33	0
Francis	5	60	19	0
Tyler	4	70	40	0
Monroe	1	33	33t	1
Solomon	1	14	14	0

PUNTING

Miami	No.	Yds.	Avg.	TB	Long
Roby	6	236	39.3	0	51
San Francisco					
Runager	3	98	32.7	0	35

PUNT RETURNS

Miami	No.	FC	Yds.	Long	TD
Walker	2	0	15	9	0
San Francisco					
McLemore	5	0	51	28	0

KICKOFF RETURNS

Miami	No.	Yds.	Long	TD
Walker	4	93	28	0
Hardy	2	31	16	0
Hill	1	16	16	0
San Francisco				
Harmon	2	24	23	0
Monroe	1	16	16	0
McIntyre	1	0	0	0

RUSHING

RUSHING	Att.	Yds.	Avg.	LG	TD
Tyler, Wendell	246	1,262	5.1	40	7
Craig, Roger	155	649	4.2	28	7
Harmon, Derrick	39	192	4.9	19	1
Ring, Bill	38	162	4.3	34	3
Montana, Joe	39	118	3.0	15	2
Solomon, Freddie	6	72	12.0	47	1
Cooper, Earl	3	13	4.3	7	0
Monroe, Carl	3	13	4.3	7	0
Runager, Max	1	-5	-5.0	-5	0
Cavanaugh, Matt	4	-11	-2.8	-1	0
49ers	534	2,465	4.6	47	21
OPPONENTS	432	1,795	4.2	25	10

RECEIVING

RECEIVING	No.	Yds	Avg.	LG	TD
Craig, Roger	71	675	9.5	64t	3
Clark, Dwight	52	880	16.9	80t	6
Cooper, Earl	41	459	11.2	26	4
Solomon, Freddie	40	737	18.4	64t	10
Tyler, Wendell	28	230	8.2	26t	2
Francis, Russ	23	285	12.4	32	2
Nehemiah, Renaldo	18	357	19.8	59t	2
Wilson, Mike	17	245	14.4	44	1
Monroe, Carl	11	139	12.6	47	1
Frank, John	7	60	8.6	21	1
Ring, Bill	3	10	3.3	15	0
Harmon, Derrick	1	2	2.0	2	0
49ers	744	5,874	7.9	80t	32
OPPONENTS	298	3,744	12.6	61	14

INTERCEPTIONS

INTERCEPTIONS	No.	Yds	Avg.	LG	TD
Turner, Keena	4	51	12.8	21	0
Lott, Ronnie	4	26	6.5	15	0
Shell, Todd	3	81	27.0	53t	1
Hicks, Dwight	3	42	14.0	29	0
McLemore, Dana	2	54	27.0	54t	1
Williamson, Carlton	2	42	21.0	26	0
Fahnhorst, Jim	2	9	4.5	9	0
Wright, Eric	2	0	0.0	0	0
Fuller, Jeff	1	38	38.0	38	0
Bunz, Dan	1	2	2.0	2	0
Clark, Mario	1	0	0.0	0	0
49ers	25	345	13.8	54t	2
OPPONENTS	10	155	15.5	43	0

KICKOFF RETURNS

KICKOFF RETURNS	No.	Yds	Avg.	LG	TD
Monroe, Carl	27	561	20.8	44	0
Harmon, Derrick	13	357	27.5	51	0
McLemore, Dana	3	80	26.7	50	0
Ring, Bill	1	27	27.0	27	0
Wilson, Mike	1	14	14.0	14	0
Cooper, Earl	1	0	0.0	0	0
McIntyre, Guy	1	0	0.0	0	0
49ers	47	1,039	22.1	51	0
OPPONENTS	78	1,499	19.2	38	0

PUNT RETURNS

PUNT RETURNS	No.	FC	Yds	Avg.	LG	TD
McLemore, Dana	31	6	331	10.7	56t	1
49ers	31	6	331	10.7	56t	1
OPPONENTS	30	4	190	6.3	25	0

PUNTING

PUNTING	No.	Yds	Avg.	TB	I-20	LG	Blk
Runager, Max	56	2,341	41.8	12	18	59	0
Orosz, Tom	5	195	39.0	0	1	55	0
49ers	61	2,536	41.6	12	19	59	0
OPPONENTS	80	3,239	40.5	4	13	58	0

SCORING

SCORING	TD	PAT	FG	S	PTS
Wersching, Ray	0	56/56	25/35	0	131
Solomon, Freddie	11	0/0	0/0	0	66
Craig, Roger	10	0/0	0/0	0	60
Tyler, Wendell	9	0/0	0/0	0	54
Clark, Dwight	6	0/0	0/0	0	36
Cooper, Eart	4	0/0	0/0	0	24
Ring, Bill	3	0/0	0/0	0	18
Francis, Russ	2	0/0	0/0	0	12
McLemore, Dana	2	0/0	0/0	0	12
Montana, Joe	2	0/0	0/0	0	12
Nehemiah, Renaldo	2	0/0	0/0	0	12
Johnson, Gary	1	0/0	0/0	1	8
Frank, John	1	0/0	0/0	0	6
Harmon, Derrick	1	0/0	0/0	0	6
Monroe, Carl	1	0/0	0/0	0	6
Shell, Todd	1	0/0	0/0	0	6
Wilson, Mike	1	0/0	0/0	0	6
49ers	57	56/56	25/35	1	475
OPPONENTS	24	24/24	19/25	1	227

PASSING

PASSING	Att.	Comp.	Pct.	Yds	LG	TD	Int	QB
Montana, Joe	432	279	64.6	3,630	80t	28	10	102.9
Cavanaugh, Matt	61	33	54.1	449	51t	4	0	99.7
Harmon, Derrick	2	0	0.0	0	0	0	0	39.6
Clark, Dwight	1	0	0.0	0	0	0	0	39.6
49ers	496	312	62.9	4,079	80t	32	10	101.9
OPPONENTS	546	298	54.6	3,744	61	14	25	65.6

Rookies indicated in italic

1984 TEAM STATISTICS

	49ers	Opp.
TOTAL FIRST DOWNS	356	302
By Rushing	138	101
By Passing	204	173
By Penalties	14	28
TOTAL YARDS GAINED	6,366	5,176
By Rushing	2,465	1,795
By Passing	3,901	3,381
TOTAL PLAYS FROM SCRIMMAGE	1,057	1,029
Rushes	534	432
Average Gain Per Rush	4.6	4.2

	49ers	Opp.
NET YARDS PASSING	3,901	3,381
Passes Attempted	496	546
Passes Completed	312	298
Percent Completed	62.9	54.6
Had Intercepted	10	25
Times Sacked	27	51
Lost Attempting to Pass	178	363
PUNTS	62	80
Total Yardage of Punts	2,536	3,239
Average Length	40.9	40.5
KICKOFFS	47	78
Total Yards Returned	1,039	1,499
Average Length of Return	22.1	19.2
PENALTIES	100	91
Yards Penalized	884	723

	49ers	Opp.
FUMBLES	26	28
Own Fumbles Recovered	14	15
Oppnts' Fumbles Recovered	13	12
FIELD GOALS	25	19
Field Goals Attempted	35	25
TOTAL POINTS SCORED	475	227
Touchdowns Scored	57	24
Touchdowns Rushing	21	10
Touchdowns Passing	32	14
Touchdown Returns	4	0
Extra Points	56	19
Safeties	1	1
AVG. TIME OF POSSESSION	30:26	29:34

SUPER BOWL XXIII SAN FRANCISCO 20, CINCINNATI 16

JANUARY 22, 1989 JOE ROBBIE STADIUM, MIAMI, FLORIDA MVP: JERRY RICE, WR

For the first 44 minutes of Super Bowl XXIII, the 49ers and the Bengals managed to produce a lot of hard hitting and a lot of field goals. The game was tied at 3-3 and 6-6 before Stanford Jennings' 93-yard kickoff return gave the Bengals a touchdown and a 13-6 lead. Then the fun began. Joe Montana engineered an 85-yard drive that tied the score, and Boomer Esiason directed the Bengals 46 yards to set up Jim Breech's third field goal. Cincinnati led 16-13. On the ensuing kickoff, a penalty backed up the

49ers to their 8-yard line, with 3:10 left in the game. Across the next 11 plays, Montana manufactured a drive that covered 92 yards, produced a victory, and likely secured him a spot in the Pro Football Hall of Fame. On the game-winning possession, during which the 49ers overcame a 10-yard penalty, Montana completed 8 of 9 passes for 97 yards, climaxed by a 10-yard pass to John Taylor with 34 seconds left. Jerry Rice's 215 receiving yards established a Super Bowl record. He was selected the game's MVP.

STARTING LINEUPS

Cincinnati (AFC)	Offense	San Francisco (NFC)
Tim McGee	WR	John Taylor
Anthony Muñoz	LT	Steve Wallace
Bruce Reimers	LG	Jesse Sapolu
Bruce Kozerski	C	Randy Cross
Max Montoya	RG	Guy McIntyre
Brian Blados	RT	Harris Barton
Rodney Holman	TE	John Frank
Eddie Brown	WR	Jerry Rice
Boomer Esiason	QB	Joe Montana
James Brooks	RB	Roger Craig
Ickey Woods	RB	Tom Rathman
	Defense	
Jim Skow	LE	Larry Roberts
Tim Krumrie	NT	Michael Carter
Jason Buck	RE	Kevin Fagan
Leon White	LOLB	Charles Haley
Carl Zander	LILB	Jim Fahnhorst
Joe Kelly	RILB	Michael Walter
Reggie Williams	ROLB	Keena Turner
Lewis Billups	LCB	Tim McKyer
Eric Thomas	RCB	Don Griffin
David Fulcher	SS	Jeff Fuller
Solomon Wilcots	FS	Ronnie Lott

SUBSTITUTIONS

Cincinnati–Offense: K–Jim Breech. P–Lee Johnson. QB–Turk Schonert. RB–Stanford Jennings, Marc Logan. WR–Cris Collinsworth, Ira Hillary, Carl Parker. TE–Jim Riggs. G–Jim Rourke. T–Dave Smith. **Defense:** DE–Eddie Edwards, Skip McClendon. DT–David Grant. LB–Leo Barker, Ed Brady, Emanuel King. CB–Rickey Dixon, Ray Horton, Daryl Smith. S–Barney Bussey. DNP: QB–Mike Norseth.
San Francisco–Offense: K–Mike Cofer. P–Barry Helton. RB–Del Rodgers, Harry Sydney. WR–Terry Greer, Mike Wilson. TE–Ron Heller, Brent Jones. C–Chuck Thomas. G–Bruce Collie. T–Bubba Paris. **Defense:** DE–Pierce Holt, Pete Kugler, Jeff Stover, Danny Stubbs. LB–Riki Ellison, Sam Kennedy, Bill Romanowski. CB–Darryl Pollard, Eric Wright. S–Greg Cox, Tom Holmoe. DNP: QB–Steve Young.

SCORING

Cincinnati	0	3	10	3	—	16
San Francisco	3	0	3	14	—	20

SF–FG Cofer 41
Cin–FG Breech 34
Cin–FG Breech 43
SF–FG Cofer 32
Cin–Jennings 93 kickoff return (Breech kick)
SF–Rice 14 pass from Montana (Cofer kick)
Cin–FG Breech 40
SF–Taylor 10 pass from Montana (Cofer kick)
Attendance–75,129

FINAL TEAM STATISTICS

	Bengals	49ers
TOTAL FIRST DOWNS	13	23
Rushing	7	6
Passing	6	16
Penalty	0	1
TOTAL NET YARDAGE	229	453
Total Offensive Plays	58	67
Average Gain per Offensive Play	3.9	6.8
NET YARDS RUSHING	106	112
Total Rushing Plays	28	27
Average Gain per Rushing Play	3.8	4.1
NET YARDS PASSING	123	341
Pass Att.–Comp.–Int.	25–11–1	36–23–0
Times Sacked–Yards Lost	5–21	4–16
Gross Yards Passing	144	357
Avg. Gain per Pass (Incl. Sacks)	4.1	8.5
PUNTS–YARDS	5–221	4–148
Average Distance	44.2	37.0
Had Blocked	0	0
TOTAL RETURN YARDAGE	137	133
Kickoff Returns–Yards	3–132	5–77
Punt Returns–Yards	2–5	3–56
Interception Returns–Yards	0–0	1–0
TOTAL TURNOVERS	1	1
Had Intercepted	1	0
Fumbles–Lost	1–0	4–1
PENALTIES–YARDS	7–65	4–32
TOTAL POINTS SCORED	16	20
Touchdowns Rushing	0	0
Touchdowns Passing	0	2
Touchdowns Returns	1	0
Extra Points	1	2
Field Goals–Attempts	3–3	2–4
Safeties	0	0
THIRD–DOWN EFFICIENCY	4/13	4/13
FOURTH–DOWN EFFICIENCY	0/1	0/0
TIME OF POSSESSION	32:43	27:17

INDIVIDUAL STATISTICS

RUSHING

Cincinnati	No.	Yds.	Avg.	Long	TD
Woods	20	79	4.0	10	0
Brooks	6	24	4.0	11	0
Jennings	1	3	3.0	3	0
Esiason	1	0	0.0	0	0
San Francisco					
Craig	17	71	4.2	13	0
Rathman	5	23	4.6	11	0
Montana	4	13	3.3	11	0
Rice	1	5	5.0	5	0

PASSING

Cincinnati	Att.	Comp.	Yds.	Long	TD	Int.
Esiason	25	11	144	23	0	1
San Francisco						
Montana	36	23	357	44	2	0

RECEIVING

Cincinnati	No.	Yds.	Long	TD
Brown	4	44	17	0
Collinsworth	3	40	23	0
McGee	2	23	18	0
Brooks	1	20	20	0
Hillary	1	17	17	0
San Francisco				
Rice	11	215	44	1
Craig	8	101	40	0
Frank	2	15	8	0
Rathman	1	16	16	0
Taylor	1	10	10t	1

PUNTING

Cincinnati	No.	Yds.	Avg.	TB	Long
Johnson	5	221	44.2	0	63
San Francisco					
Helton	4	148	37.0	0	55

PUNT RETURNS

Cincinnati	No.	FC	Yds.	Long	TD
Horton	1	0	5	5	0
Hillary	1	0	0	0	0
San Francisco					
Taylor	3	1	56	45	0

KICKOFF RETURNS

Cincinnati	No.	Yds.	Long	TD
Jennings	2	117	93t	1
San Francisco				
Rodgers	3	53	22	0
Taylor	1	13	13	0
Sydney	1	11	11	0

1988 Individual Statistics

RUSHING	Att.	Yds.	Avg.	LG	TD
Craig, Roger	310	1,502	4.9	46t	9
Rathman, Tom	102	427	4.2	26	2
Young, Steve	27	184	6.8	49t	1
Montana, Joe	38	132	3.5	15	3
DuBose, Doug	24	116	4.8	37t	2
Rice, Jerry	13	107	8.2	29	1
Sydney, Harry	9	50	5.6	13	0
Flagler, Terrence	3	5	1.7	4	0
Helton, Barry	1	0	0.0	0	0
49ers	**527**	**2,523**	**4.8**	**49t**	**18**
OPPONENTS	**441**	**1,588**	**3.6**	**36t**	**8**

RECEIVING	No.	Yds	Avg.	LG	TD
Craig, Roger	76	492	6.5	22	1
Rice, Jerry	64	1,078	16.8	96t	9
Rathman, Tom	42	329	7.8	24	0
Wilson, Mike	33	450	13.6	31	3
Frank, John	16	296	18.5	38	3
Taylor, John	14	325	23.2	73t	2
Heller, Ron	14	140	10.0	22	0
Greer, Terry	8	120	15.0	31	0
Jones, Brent	8	57	7.1	18t	2
DuBose, Doug	6	57	9.5	13	0
Flagler, Terrence	4	72	18.0	57	0
Chandler, Wes	4	33	8.3	9	0
Sydney, Harry	2	18	9.0	9	0
McIntyre, Guy	1	17	17.0	17t	1
Nicholas, Calvin	1	14	14.0	14	0
49ers	**293**	**3,498**	**11.9**	**96t**	**21**
OPPONENTS	**292**	**3,284**	**11.3**	**67t**	**25**

INTERCEPTIONS	No.	Yds	Avg.	LG	TD
McKyer, Tim	7	11	1.6	7	0
Lott, Ronnie	5	59	11.8	44	0
Fuller, Jeff	4	18	4.5	10	0
Holmoe, Tom	2	0	0.0	0	0
Wright, Eric	2	-2	-1.0	0	0
Turner, Keena	1	2	2.0	2	0
Carter, Michael	1	0	0.0	0	0
49ers	**22**	**88**	**4.0**	**44**	**0**
OPPONENTS	**14**	**185**	**13.2**	**47t**	**1**

KICKOFF RETURNS	No.	Yds	Avg.	LG	TD
DuBose, Doug	32	608	19.0	44	0
Taylor, John	12	225	18.8	29	0
Rodgers, Del	6	98	16.3	24	0
Craig, Roger	2	32	16.0	17	0
Sydney, Harry	1	8	8.0	8	0
Thomas, Chuck	1	5	5.0	5	0
Wilson, Mike	1	2	2.0	2	0
49ers	**55**	**978**	**17.8**	**44**	**0**
OPPONENTS	**73**	**1,,362**	**18.6**	**40**	**1**

PUNT RETURNS	No.	FC	Yds	Avg.	LG	TD
Taylor, John	44	7	556	12.6	95t	2
Chandler, Wes	6	5	28	4.7	13	0
Griffin, Don	4	3	28	7.0	10	0
49ers	**54**	**15**	**612**	**11.3**	**95t**	**2**
OPPONENTS	**47**	**10**	**426**	**9.1**	**41**	**0**

PUNTING	No.	Yds	Avg.	TB	I-20	LG	Blk
Helton, Barry	78	3,069	39.4	5	22	53	1
Runager, Max	1	24	24.0	0	0	24	0
49ers	**79**	**3,093**	**39.2**	**5**	**22**	**53**	**1**
OPPONENTS	**86**	**3,522**	**41.0**	**5**	**21**	**57**	**0**

SCORING	TD	PAT	FG	S	PTS
Cofer, Mike	0	40/41	27/38	0	121
Craig, Roger	10	0/0	0/0	0	60
Rice, Jerry	10	0/0	0/0	0	60
Taylor, John	4	0/0	0/0	0	24
Frank, John	3	0/0	0/0	0	18
Montana, Joe	3	0/0	0/0	0	18
Wilson, Mike	3	0/0	0/0	0	18
DuBose, Doug	2	0/0	0/0	0	12
Jones, Brent	2	0/0	0/0	0	12
Rathman, Tom	2	0/0	0/0	0	12
McIntyre, Guy	1	0/0	0/0	0	6
Young, Steve	1	0/0	0/0	0	6
Haley, Charles	0	0/0	0/0	1	2
49ers	**41**	**40/41**	**27/38**	**1**	**369**
OPPONENTS	**34**	**34/34**	**18/24**	**1**	**294**

PASSING	Att.	Comp.	Pct.	Yds	LG	TD	Int	QB
Montana, Joe	397	238	60.0	2,981	96t	18	10	87.9
Young, Steve	101	54	53.5	680	73t	3	3	72.2
Rice, Jerry	3	1	33.3	14	14	0	1	9.7
Sydney, Harry	1	0	0.0	0	0	0	0	39.6
49ers	**502**	**293**	**58.4**	**3,675**	**96t**	**21**	**14**	**83.5**
OPPONENTS	**530**	**292**	**55.1**	**3,284**	**67t**	**25**	**22**	**72.2**

Rookies indicated in italic

1988 Team Statistics

	49ers	Opp.
TOTAL FIRST DOWNS	326	277
By Rushing	141	90
By Passing	167	160
By Penalties	18	27
TOTAL YARDS GAINED	5,900	4,575
By Rushing	2,523	1,588
By Passing	3,377	2,987
TOTAL PLAYS		
FROM SCRIMMAGE	1,076	1,013
Rushes	527	441
Average Gain Per Rush	4.8	3.6

NET YARDS PASSING	3,377	2,987
Passes Attempted	502	530
Passes Completed	293	292
Percent Completed	58.4	55.1
Had Intercepted	14	22
Times Sacked	47	42
Lost Attempting to Pass	298	297
PUNTS	80	86
Total Yardage of Punts	3,093	3,522
Average Length	38.7	41.0
KICKOFFS	55	73
Total Yards Returned	978	1,362
Average Length of Return	17.8	18.7
PENALTIES	115	76
Yards Penalized	986	603

FUMBLES	27	30
Own Fumbles Recovered	15	16
Oppnts' Fumbles Recovered	14	12
FIELD GOALS	27	18
Field Goals Attempted	38	24
TOTAL POINTS SCORED	369	294
Touchdowns Scored	41	34
Touchdowns Rushing	18	8
Touchdowns Passing	21	25
Touchdown Returns	2	1
Extra Points	40	34
Safeties	1	1
AVG. TIME OF POSSESSION	30:31	29:29

The 49ers needed last-minute heroics to win the previous Super Bowl. In game XXIV, the outcome never was in doubt. While new coach George Seifert calmly patrolled San Francisco's sideline, his offense methodically produced 4 touchdowns in its first 6 possessions. Quarterback Joe Montana directed drives of 66, 54, 69, and 59 yards while building up a halftime lead of 27-3. When the second half began, the rout resumed, as the 49ers intercepted John Elway on back-to-back possessions, and quickly turned

each turnover into another touchdown. With more than 24 minutes left, the 49ers owned an insurmountable 41-3 advantage. Joe Montana finished the game with a Super Bowl-record 5 touchdown passes and earned MVP honors for an unprecedented third time. The 49ers became the first team to repeat as champions since the Pittsburgh Steelers of games XIII and XIV. Broncos coach Dan Reeves was suitably impressed: "The 49ers are playing at a level that's incredible."

STARTING LINEUPS

Denver (AFC)	Offense	San Francisco (NFC)
Vance Johnson	WR	John Taylor
Gerald Perry	LT	Bubba Paris
Jim Juriga	LG	Guy McIntyre
Keith Kartz	C	Jesse Sapolu
Doug Widell	RG	Bruce Collie
Ken Lanier	RT	Harris Barton
Orson Mobley	TE	Brent Jones
Mark Jackson	WR	Jerry Rice
John Elway	QB	Joe Montana
Steve Sewell	RB	Roger Craig
Bobby Humphrey	RB	Tom Rathman
Defense		
Alphonso Carreker	LE	Pierce Holt
Greg Kragen	NT	Michael Carter
Ron Holmes	RE	Kevin Fagan
Michael Brooks	LOLB	Charles Haley
Rick Dennison	LILB	Matt Millen
Karl Mecklenburg	RILB	Michael Walter
Simon Fletcher	ROLB	Keena Turner
Tyrone Braxton	LCB	Darryl Pollard
Wymon Henderson	RCB	Don Griffin
Dennis Smith	SS	Chet Brooks
Steve Atwater	FS	Ronnie Lott

SUBSTITUTIONS

Denver—Offense: K–David Treadwell. P–Mike Horan. QB–Gary Kubiak. RB–Ken Bell, Melvin Bratton, Sammy Winder. WR–Ricky Nattiel, Michael Young. TE–Paul Green, Clarence Kay. C–Keith Bishop. G–Monte Smith. **Defense:** DE–Warren Powers, Andre Townsend. NT–Brad Henke. LB–Scott Curtis, Bruce Klostermann, Tim Lucas, Marc Munford. CB–Darren Carrington, Mark Haynes. S–Kip Corrington, Randy Robbins.
San Francisco—Offense: K–Mike Cofer. P–Barry Helton. QB–Steve Young. RB–Terrence Flagler, Harry Sydney, Spencer Tillman. WR–Mike Sherrard, Mike Wilson. TE–Wesley Walls, Jamie Williams. C–Chuck Thomas. T–Steve Wallace. G–Terry Tausch. **Defense:** DE–Larry Roberts, Danny Stubbs. NT–Jim Burt, Pete Kugler. LB–Keith DeLong, Steve Hendrickson, Bill Romanowski. CB–Tim McKyer, Eric Wright. S–Johnny Jackson.

SCORING

San Francisco	13	14	14	14	—	55
Denver	3	0	7	0	—	10

SF–Rice 20 pass from Montana (Cofer kick)
Den–FG Treadwell 42
SF–Jones 7 pass from Montana (kick failed)
SF–Rathman 1 run (Cofer kick)
SF–Rice 38 pass from Montana (Cofer kick)
SF–Rice 28 pass from Montana (Cofer kick)
SF–Taylor 35 pass from Montana (Cofer kick)
Den–Elway 3 run (Treadwell kick)
SF–Rathman 3 run (Cofer kick)
SF–Craig 1 run (Cofer kick)
Attendance–72,919

FINAL TEAM STATISTICS

	49ers	Broncos
TOTAL FIRST DOWNS	28	12
Rushing	14	5
Passing	14	6
Penalty	0	1
TOTAL NET YARDAGE	461	167
Total Offensive Plays	77	52
Average Gain per Offensive Play	6.0	3.2
NET YARDS RUSHING	144	64
Total Rushing Plays	44	17
Average Gain per Rushing Play	3.3	3.8
NET YARDS PASSING	317	103
Pass Att.–Comp.–Int.	32-24-0	29-11-2
Times Sacked–Yards Lost	1-0	6-33
Gross Yards Passing	317	136
Avg. Gain per Pass (Incl. Sacks)	9.6	2.9
PUNTS–YARDS	4-158	6-231
Average Distance	39.5	38.5
Had Blocked	0	0
TOTAL RETURN YARDAGE	129	207
Kickoff Returns–Yards	3-49	9-196
Punt Returns–Yards	3-38	2-11
Interception Returns–Yards	2-42	0-0
TOTAL TURNOVERS	0	4
Fumbles–Lost	0-0	3-2
Had Intercepted	0	2
PENALTIES–YARDS	4-38	0-0
TOTAL POINTS SCORED	55	10
Touchdowns Rushing	3	1
Touchdowns Passing	5	0
Touchdowns Returns	0	0
Extra Points	7	1
Field Goals–Attempts	0-0	1-1
Safeties	0	0
THIRD–DOWN EFFICIENCY	8/15	3/11
FOURTH–DOWN EFFICIENCY	2/2	0/0
TIME OF POSSESSION	39:31	20:29

INDIVIDUAL STATISTICS

RUSHING

Denver	No.	Yds.	Avg.	Long	TD
Humphrey	12	61	5.1	34	0
Elway	4	8	2.0	3t	1
Winder	1	–5	–5.0	–5	0
San Francisco					
Craig	20	69	3.5	18	1
Rathman	11	38	3.5	18	2
Montana	2	15	7.5	10	0
Flagler	6	14	2.3	10	0
S. Young	4	6	1.5	11	0
Sydney	1	2	2.0	2	0

PASSING

Denver	Att.	Comp.	Yds.	Long	TD	Int.
Elway	26	10	108	27	0	2
Kubiak	3	1	28	28	0	0
San Francisco						
Montana	29	22	297	38t	5	0
S. Young	3	2	20	13	0	0

RECEIVING

Denver	No.	Yds.	Long	TD
Humphrey	3	38	27	0
Sewell	2	22	12	0
Johnson	2	21	13	0
Nattiel	1	28	28	0
Bratton	1	14	14	0
Winder	1	7	7	0
Kay	1	6	6	0
San Francisco				
Rice	7	148	38t	3
Craig	5	34	12	0
Rathman	4	43	18	0
Taylor	3	49	35t	1
Sherrard	1	13	13	0
Walls	1	9	9	0
Jones	1	7	7t	1
Sydney	1	7	7	0
Williams	1	7	7	0

PUNTING

Denver	No.	Yds.	Avg.	TB	Long
Horan	6	231	38.5	0	43
San Francisco					
Helton	4	158	39.5	0	47

PUNT RETURNS

Denver	No.	FC	Yds.	Long	TD
Johnson	2	1	11	7	0
San Francisco					
Taylor	3	2	38	17	0

KICKOFF RETURNS

Denver	No.	Yds.	Long	TD
Carrington	6	146	39	0
Bell	2	41	24	0
Bratton	1	9	9	0
San Francisco				
Flagler	3	49	22	0

RUSHING	Att.	Yds	Avg.	LG	TD
Craig, Roger	271	1,054	3.9	27	6
Rathman, Tom	79	305	3.9	13	1
Montana, Joe	49	227	4.6	19	3
Flagler, Terrence	33	129	3.9	29t	1
Young, Steve	38	126	3.3	22	2
Sydney, Harry	9	56	6.2	18	0
Rice, Jerry	5	33	6.6	17	0
Henderson, Keith	7	30	4.3	11t	1
Taylor, John	1	6	6.0	6	0
Helton, Barry	1	0	0.0	0	0
49ers	493	1,966	4.0	29t	14
OPPONENTS	372	1,383	3.7	23	9

RECEIVING	No.	Yds	Avg.	LG	TD
Rice, Jerry	82	1,483	18.1	68t	17
Rathman, Tom	73	616	8.4	36	1
Taylor, John	60	1,077	18.0	95t	10
Craig, Roger	49	473	9.7	44	1
Jones, Brent	40	500	12.5	36t	4
Wilson, Mike	9	103	11.4	19	1
Sydney, Harry	9	71	7.9	13	0
Flagler, Terrence	6	51	8.5	30	0
Walls, Wesley	4	16	4.0	9	1
Henderson, Keith	3	130	43.3	78	0
Williams, Jamie	3	38	12.7	17	0
Greer, Terry	1	26	26.0	26	0
49ers	339	4,584	13.5	95t	35
OPPONENTS	316	3,568	11.3	65t	15

INTERCEPTIONS	No.	Yds	Avg.	LG	TD
Lott, Ronnie	5	34	6.8	28	0
Brooks, Chet	3	31	10.3	19	0
Wright, Eric	2	37	18.5	23	0
Jackson, Johnny	2	35	17.5	19	0
Griffn, Don	2	6	3.0	3	0
Turner, Keena	1	42	42.0	42	0
Holmoe, Tom	1	23	23.0	23	0
McKyer, Tim	1	18	18.0	18	0
Romanowski, Bill	1	13	13.0	13	0
Pollard, Darryl	1	12	12.0	12	0
Millen, Matt	1	10	10.0	10	0
DeLong, Keith	1	1	1.0	1	0
49ers	21	262	12.4	42	0
OPPONENTS	11	140	12.7	35	0

KICKOFF RETURNS	No.	Yds	Avg.	LG	TD
Flagler, Terrence	32	643	20.1	41	0
Tillman, Spencer	10	206	20.6	60	0
Sydney, Harry	3	16	5.3	16	0
Taylor, John	2	51	25.5	27	0
Henderson, Keith	2	21	10.5	13	0
Greer, Terry	1	17	17.0	17	0
Jackson, Johnny	1	0	0.0	0	0
49ers	51	954	18.7	60	0
OPPONENTS	76	1,435	18.9	37	0

PUNT RETURNS	No.	FC	Yds	Avg.	LG	TD
Taylor, John	36	20	417	11.6	37	0
Greer, Terry	1	0	3	3.0	3	0
Griffin, Don	1	0	9	9.0	9	0
Romanowski, Bill	1	0	0	0.0	0	0
49ers	39	20	429	11.0	37	0
OPPONENTS	35	4	361	10.3	22	0

PUNTING	No.	Yds	Avg.	TB	I-20	LG	Blk
Helton, Barry	55	2226	40.5	6	13	56	1
49ers	56	2226	39.8	6	13	56	1
OPPONENTS	74	2875	38.9	4	18	57	0

SCORING	TD	PAT	FG	S	PTS
Cofer, Mike	0	49/51	29/36	0	136
Rice, Jerry	17	0/0	0/0	0	102
Taylor, John	10	0/0	0/0	0	60
Craig, Roger	7	0/0	0/0	0	42
Jones, Brent	4	0/0	0/0	0	24
Montana, Joe	3	0/0	0/0	0	18
Rathman, Tom	2	0/0	0/0	0	12
Young, Steve	2	0/0	0/0	0	12
Flagler, Terrence	1	0/0	0/0	0	6
Haley, Charles	1	0/0	0/0	0	6
Henderson, Keith	1	0/0	0/0	0	6
Jackson, Johnny	1	0/0	0/0	0	6
Walls, Wesley	1	0/0	0/0	0	6
Wilson, Mike	1	0/0	0/0	0	6
49ERS	51	49/51	29/36	0	442
OPPONENTS	26	26/26	23/31	1	253

PASSING	Att.	Comp.	Pct.	Yds	LG	TD	Int	QB
Montana, Joe	386	271	70.2	3,521	95t	26	8	112.4
Young, Steve	92	64	69.6	1,001	50t	8	3	120.8
Bono, Steve	5	4	80.0	62	45t	1	0	157.9
49ers	483	339	70.2	4,584	95t	35	11	114.8
OPPONENTS	564	316	56.0	3,568	65t	15	21	68.5

Rookies indicated in italic

1989 Team Statistics

	49ers	Opp.
TOTAL FIRST DOWNS	350	283
By Rushing	124	76
By Passing	209	178
By Penalties	17	29
TOTAL YARDS GAINED	6,268	4,618
By Rushing	1,966	1,383
By Passing	4,302	3,235
TOTAL PLAYS FROM SCRIMMAGE	1,021	979
Rushes	493	372
Average Gain Per Rush	4.0	3.7

	49ers	Opp.
NET YARDS PASSING	4,302	3,235
Passes Attempted	483	564
Passes Completed	339	316
Percent Completed	70.2	56.0
Had Intercepted	11	21
Times Sacked	45	43
Lost Attempting to Pass	282	333
PUNTS	56	74
Total Yardage of Punts	2,226	2,875
Average Length	39.8	38.9
KICKOFFS	51	76
Total Yards Returned	954	1,435
Average Length of Return	18.7	18.9
PENALTIES	109	75
Yards Penalized	922	581

	49ers	Opp.
FUMBLES	32	34
Own Fumbles Recovered	18	18
Oppnts' Fumbles Recovered	16	14
FIELD GOALS	29	23
Field Goals Attempted	36	31
TOTAL POINTS SCORED	442	253
Touchdowns Scored	51	26
Touchdowns Rushing	14	9
Touchdowns Passing	35	15
Touchdown Returns	2	2
Extra Points	49	26
Safeties	0	1
AVG. TIME OF POSSESSION	31:45	28:15

Quarterback Steve Young, who had labored in Joe Montana's shadow throughout most of his NFL career, staked his claim to the spotlight with a record-setting performance in a 49-26 victory over the San Diego Chargers. On just the third play from scrimmage, Young gave an indication of things to come when he connected with Jerry Rice on a 44-yard touchdown pass. San Francisco scored on each of its first three possessions—and four of its first five—as it raced to a commanding 28-10 halftme lead that all but

sealed the Chargers' fate. By game's end, Young had completed 24 of 36 passes for 325 yards and a Super Bowl-record 6 touchdown passes, eclipsing the mark set by Montana in game XXIV. Young also was the game's leading rusher with 49 yards on 5 attempts. As he stood on the sideline near game's end, Young playfully asked a teammate to help him remove the monkey from his back—a reference to the oft-repeated reminder that he never had led his team to a Super Bowl victory.

STARTING LINEUPS

San Diego (AFC)	Offense	San Francisco (NFC)
Shawn Jefferson	WR	John Taylor
Harry Swayne	LT	Steve Wallace
Isaac Davis	LG	Jesse Sapolu
Courtney Hall	C	Bart Oates
Joe Cocozzo	RG	Derrick Deese
Stan Brock	RT	Harris Barton
Duane Young	TE	Brent Jones
Mark Seay	WR	Jerry Rice
Stan Humphries	QB	Steve Young
Natrone Means	RB	Ricky Watters
Alfred Pupunu	TE–RB	William Floyd
	Defense	
Chris Mims	LE	Dennis Brown
Shawn Lee	LT	Bryant Young
Reuben Davis	RT	Dana Stubblefield
Leslie O'Neal	RE	Rickey Jackson
David Griggs	LLB	Lee Woodall
Dennis Gibson	MLB	Gary Plummer
Junior Seau	RLB	Ken Norton
Darrien Gordon	LCB	Eric Davis
Dwayne Harper	RCB	Deion Sanders
Darren Carrington	SS	Tim McDonald
Stanley Richard	FS	Merton Hanks

SUBSTITUTIONS

San Diego–Offense: K–John Carney. P–Bryan Wagner. QB–Gale Gilbert. RB–Eric Bieniemy, Rodney Culver, Ronnie Harmon. WR–Andre Coleman, Tony Martin. TE–David Binn, Shannon Mitchell. T–Eric Jonassen, Vaughn Parker. **Defense:** DT–Les Miller, John Parrella. DE–Raylee Johnson. LB–Lewis Bush, Steve Hendrickson, Doug Miller. CB–Willie Clark, Sean Vanhorse. S–Eric Castle, Rodney Harrison. **DNP:** C–Curtis Whitley. **Inactive:** QB–Jeff Brohm. WR–Johnnie Barnes. TE–Aaron Laing. G–Joe Milinichik. C–Greg Engel. DT–Reggie White. DE–Cornell Thomas. S–Lonnie Young.
San Francisco–Offense: K–Doug Brien. P–Klaus Wilmsmeyer. QB–Elvis Grbac, Bill Musgrave. RB–Dexter Carter, Marc Logan, Derek Loville, Adam Walker. WR–Ed McCaffrey, Nate Singleton. TE–Ted Popson. G–Chris Dalman, Ralph Tamm. T–Frank Pollack. **Defense:** DT–Rhett Hall. DE–Tim Harris, Charles Mann, Troy Wilson. LB–Antonio Goss, Darin Jordan, Kevin Mitchell. CB–Toi Cook, Tyrone Drakeford. S–Dana Hall. **Inactive:** TE–Brett Carolan. T–Harry Boatswain. G–Rod Milstead. DE–Richard Dent, Todd Kelly, Mark Thomas. S–Dedrick Dodge.

SCORING

San Diego	7	3	8	8	—	26
San Francisco	14	14	14	7	—	49

SF–Rice 44 pass from S. Young (Brien kick)
SF–Watters 51 pass from S. Young (Brien kick)
SD–Means 1 run (Carney kick)
SF–Floyd 5 pass from S. Young (Brien kick)
SF–Watters 8 pass from S. Young (Brien kick)
SD–FG Carney 31
SF–Watters 9 run (Brien kick)
SF–Rice 15 pass from S. Young (Brien kick)
SD–Coleman 98 kickoff return
   (Seay pass from Humphries)
SF–Rice 7 pass from S. Young (Brien kick)
SD–Martin 30 pass from Humphries
   (Pupunu pass from Humphries)
Attendance–74,107

FINAL TEAM STATISTICS

	Chargers	49ers
TOTAL FIRST DOWNS	20	28
Rushing	5	10
Passing	14	17
Penalty	1	1
TOTAL NET YARDAGE	354	449
Total Offensive Plays	76	73
Average Gain per Offensive Play	4.7	6.2
NET YARDS RUSHING	67	133
Total Rushing Plays	19	32
Average Gain per Rushing Play	3.5	4.2
NET YARDS PASSING	287	316
Pass Att.–Comp.–Int.	55–27–3	38–25–0
Times Sacked–Yards Lost	2–18	3–15
Gross Yards Passing	305	331
Avg. Gain per Pass (Incl. Sacks)	5.0	7.7
PUNTS–YARDS	4–195	5–199
Average Distance	48.8	39.8
Had Blocked	0	0
TOTAL RETURN YARDAGE	243	76
Kickoff Returns–Yards	8–242	4–48
Punt Returns–Yards	3–1	2–12
Interception Returns–Yards	0–0	3–16
TOTAL TURNOVERS	3	0
Fumbles–Lost	1–0	2–0
Had Intercepted	3	0
PENALTIES–YARDS	6–65	3–18
TOTAL POINTS SCORED	26	49
Touchdowns Rushing	1	1
Touchdowns Passing	1	6
Touchdowns Returns	1	0
Extra Points	1	7
Two-Point Conversions	2	0
Field Goal–Attempts	1–1	0–1
Safeties	0	0
THIRD–DOWN EFFICIENCY	6/16	7/13
FOURTH–DOWN EFFICIENCY	0/4	0/0
TIME OF POSSESSION	28:29	31:31

INDIVIDUAL STATISTICS

RUSHING

San Diego	No.	Yds.	Avg.	Long	TD
Means	13	33	2.5	11	1
Harmon	2	10	5.0	10	0
Jefferson	1	10	10.0	10	0
Gilbert	1	8	8.0	8	0
Bieniemy	1	3	3.0	3	0
Humphries	1	3	3.0	3	0
San Francisco					
S. Young	5	49	9.8	21	0
Watters	15	47	3.1	13	1
Floyd	9	32	3.6	6	0
Rice	1	10	10.0	10	0
Carter	2	–5	–2.5	1	0

PASSING

San Diego	Att.	Comp.	Yds.	Long	TD	Int.
Humphries	49	24	275	33	1	2
Gilbert	6	3	30	20	0	1
San Francisco						
S. Young	36	24	325	51t	6	0
Musgrave	1	1	6	6	0	0
Grbac	1	0	0	0	0	0

RECEIVING

San Diego	No.	Yds.	Long	TD
Harmon	8	68	20	0
Seay	7	75	22	0
Pupunu	4	48	23	0
Martin	3	59	30t	1
Jefferson	2	15	9	0
Bieniemy	1	33	33	0
Means	1	4	4	0
D. Young	1	3	3	0
San Francisco				
Rice	10	149	44t	3
Taylor	4	43	16	0
Floyd	4	26	9	1
Watters	3	61	51t	2
Jones	2	41	33	0
Popson	1	6	6	0
McCaffrey	1	5	5	0

PUNTING

San Diego	No.	Yds.	Avg.	TB	Long
Wagner	4	195	48.8	0	55
San Francisco					
Wilmsmeyer	5	199	39.8	0	46

PUNT RETURNS

San Diego	No.	FC	Yds.	Long	TD
Gordon	3	2	1	1	0
San Francisco					
Carter	2	0	12	11	0

KICKOFF RETURNS

San Diego	No.	Yds.	Long	TD
Coleman	8	244	98t	1
San Francisco				
Carter	4	48	18	0

1994 Individual Statistics

RUSHING	Att.	Yds	Avg.	LG	TD
Watters, Ricky	239	877	3.7	23	6
Floyd, William	87	305	3.5	26	6
Young, Steve	58	293	5.1	27	7
Logan, Marc	33	143	4.3	22	1
Loville, Derek	31	99	3.2	13	0
Rice, Jerry	7	93	13.3	28t	2
Walker, Adam	13	54	4.2	14	1
Carter, Dexter	8	34	4.3	18	0
Grbac, Elvis	13	1	0.1	6	0
Taylor, John	2	-2	-1.0	1	0
49ers	**491**	**1,897**	**3.9**	**28t**	**23**
OPPONENTS	**375**	**1,338**	**3.6**	**44t**	**16**

RECEIVING	No.	Yds	Avg.	LG	TD
Rice, Jerry	112	1,499	13.4	69t	13
Watters, Ricky	66	719	10.9	65t	5
Jones, Brent	49	670	13.7	69t	9
Taylor, John	41	531	13.0	35	5
Singleton, Nate	21	294	14.0	43t	2
Floyd, William	19	145	7.6	15	0
Logan, Marc	16	97	6.1	15	1
Popson, Ted	13	141	10.9	24	0
McCaffrey, Ed	11	131	11.9	32	2
Carter, Dexter	7	99	14.1	44	0
Loville, Derek	2	26	13.0	19	0
Carolan, Brett	2	10	5.0	6	0
49ers	**359**	**4,362**	**12.2**	**69t**	**37**
OPPONENTS	**329**	**3,756**	**11.4**	**90**	**15**

INTERCEPTIONS	No.	Yds	Avg.	LG	TD
Hanks, Merton	7	93	13.1	38	0
Sanders, Deion	6	303	50.5	93t	3
McDonald, Tim	2	79	39.5	73t	1
Hall, Dana	2	0	0.0	0	0
Cook, Toi	1	18	18.0	18	0
Davis, Eric	1	8	8.0	8	0
Drakeford, Tyronne	1	6	6.0	6	0
Plummer, Gary	1	1	1.0	1	0
Brown, Dennis	1	0	0.0	0	0
Norton, Ken, Jr.	1	0	0.0	0	0
49ers	**23**	**508**	**22.1**	**93t**	**4**
OPPONENTS	**11**	**107**	**9.7**	**36t**	**1**

KICKOFF RETURNS	No.	Yds	Avg.	LG	TD
Carter, Dexter	48	1,105	23.0	96t	1
Walker, Adam	6	82	13.7	19	0
Loville, Derek	2	34	17.0	19	0
Singleton, Nate	2	23	11.5	17	0
49ers	**58**	**1,244**	**21.5**	**96t**	**1**
OPPONENTS	**89**	**1,912**	**21.5**	**51**	**0**

PUNT RETURNS	No.	FC	Yds	Avg.	LG	TD
Carter, Dexter	38	12	321	8.5	26	0
Singleton, Nate	2	1	13	6.5	8	0
49ers	**40**	**13**	**334**	**8.4**	**26**	**0**
OPPONENTS	**28**	**10**	**242**	**8.6**	**43**	**0**

PUNTING	No.	Yds	Avg.	TB	I-20	LG	Blk
Wilmsmeyer, Klaus	54	2,235	41.4	3	18	60	0
49ers	**54**	**2,235**	**41.4**	**3**	**18**	**60**	**0**
OPPONENTS	**77**	**3,274**	**42.5**	**9**	**19**	**65**	**0**

SCORING	TD	PAT	FG	S	PTS
Brien, Doug	0	60/62	15/20	0	150
Rice, Jerry	15	0/0	0/0	0	92
Watters, Ricky	11	0/0	0/0	0	66
Jones, Brent	9	0/0	0/0	0	56
Young, Steve	7	0/0	0/0	0	42
Floyd, William	6	0/0	0/0	0	36
Taylor, John	5	0/0	0/0	0	30
Sanders, Deion	3	0/0	0/0	0	18
Logan, Marc	2	0/0	0/0	0	12
McCaffrey, Ed	2	0/0	0/0	0	12
McDonald, Tim	2	0/0	0/0	0	12
Singleton, Nate	2	0/0	0/0	0	12
Carter, Dexter	1	0/0	0/0	0	6
Walker, Adam	1	0/0	0/0	0	6
49ers	**66**	**60/62**	**15/20**	**0**	**505**
OPPONENTS	**35**	**23/23**	**15/21**	**2**	**296**

PASSING	Att.	Comp.	Pct.	Yds	LG	TD	Int	QB
Young, Steve	461	324	70.3	3,969	69t	35	10	112.8
Grbac, Elvis	50	35	70.0	393	42	2	1	98.2
49ERS	**511**	**359**	**70.3**	**4,362**	**69t**	**37**	**11**	**111.4**
OPPONENTS	**583**	**329**	**56.4**	**3,756**	**90**	**15**	**23**	**68.1**

Rookies indicated in italic

1994 Team Statistics

	49ers	Opp.
TOTAL FIRST DOWNS	362	285
By Rushing	122	82
By Passing	210	182
By Penalties	30	21
TOTAL YARDS GAINED	6,060	4,839
By Rushing	1,897	1,338
By Passing	4,163	3,501
TOTAL PLAYS		
FROM SCRIMMAGE	1,037	996
Rushes	491	375
Average Gain Per Rush	3.9	3.6

NET YARDS PASSING	4,163	3,501
Passes Attempted	511	583
Passes Completed	359	329
Percent Completed	70.3	56.4
Had Intercepted	11	23
Times Sacked	35	38
Lost Attempting to Pass	199	255
PUNTS	54	77
Total Yardage of Punts	2,235	3,274
Average Length	41.4	42.5
KICKOFFS	58	89
Total Yards Returned	1,244	1,912
Average Length of Return	21.4	21.5
PENALTIES	109	108
Yards Penalized	890	912

FUMBLES	25	25
Own Fumbles Recovered	12	13
Oppnts' Fumbles Recovered	12	13
FIELD GOALS	15	15
Field Goals Attempted	20	21
TOTAL POINTS SCORED	505	296
Touchdowns Scored	66	35
Touchdowns Rushing	23	16
Touchdowns Passing	37	15
Touchdown Returns	6	4
Extra Points	60	23
Safeties	0	2
AVG. TIME OF POSSESSION	31:38	28:22